THE LONDON
Dennis Dart and Dart SLF

THE LONDON
Dennis Dart and Dart SLF

DAVID BEDDALL

AN IMPRINT OF PEN & SWORD BOOKS LTD.
YORKSHIRE - PHILADELPHIA

First published in Great Britain in 2022 by
Pen and Sword Transport
An imprint of
Pen & Sword Books Ltd.
Yorkshire - Philadelphia

Copyright © David Beddall, 2022

ISBN 978 1 39909 518 1

The right of David Beddall to be identified as Author of this work has been asserted by him in accordance with the Copyright, Designs and Patents Act 1988.

A CIP catalogue record for this book is available from the British Library.

All rights reserved. No part of this book may be reproduced or transmitted in any form or by any means, electronic or mechanical including photocopying, recording or by any information storage and retrieval system, without permission from the Publisher in writing.

Typeset by SJmagic DESIGN SERVICES, India.

Printed and bound by Printworks Global Ltd, London/Hong Kong.

Pen & Sword Books Ltd incorporates the imprints of Pen & Sword Books Archaeology, Atlas, Aviation, Battleground, Discovery, Family History, History, Maritime, Military, Naval, Politics, Railways, Select, Transport, True Crime, Fiction, Frontline Books, Leo Cooper, Praetorian Press, Seaforth Publishing, Wharncliffe and White Owl.

For a complete list of Pen & Sword titles please contact

PEN & SWORD BOOKS LIMITED
47 Church Street, Barnsley, South Yorkshire, S70 2AS, England
E-mail: enquiries@pen-and-sword.co.uk
Website: www.pen-and-sword.co.uk

or

PEN AND SWORD BOOKS
1950 Lawrence Rd, Havertown, PA 19083, USA
E-mail: Uspen-and-sword@casematepublishers.com
Website: www.penandswordbooks.com

CONTENTS

Acknowledgements 7
Introduction 8
London Buses Limited 10
R&I Tours 24
London Country North West 26
Metrobus 27
County Bus 36
Transcity 38
Thamesway 39
Grey Green 41
Westlink 43
Centrewest/First London 44
Stagecoach London 59
Go-Ahead London 74
Cowie London/Arriva London 84
Metroline 95
MTL London Northern 107
London United 110
Kentish Bus/Arriva Kent Thameside 122
London & Country 126
Londonlinks 128
Docklands Minibus 130

Armchair	*131*
Capital Citybus	*135*
Limebourne	*137*
Tellings-Golden Miller	*140*
F.E. Thorpe	*148*
Epsom Buses/Quality Line	*152*
Airlinks	*157*
Sovereign, Harrow	*158*
Wings Buses	*160*
Arriva the Shires & Essex	*161*
Mitcham Belle	*164*
Connex	*166*
Hackney Community Transport	*170*
Blue Triangle	*174*
Durham Travel Services	*177*
Docklands Buses	*178*
East Thames Buses	*180*
Ealing Community Transport	*182*
Travel London	*184*
Centra London	*190*
NCP Challenger	*192*
East London Bus Group	*193*
Abellio London	*195*
London Sovereign	*200*
Tower Transit	*202*
Sources	*204*

ACKNOWLEDGEMENTS

I would like to thank my wife, Helen, for her continued support through writing this book. A big thank you also goes to Liam Farrer-Beddall, David Moth, Gary Seamarks, Aethan Blake, Ian Armstrong, Jeff Lloyd and Matthew Wharmby. Without these individuals this book would be without photographs. Also, a thank you goes to Andrew Braddock for giving me an insight into the development of the Dennis Dart SLF.

INTRODUCTION

Remaining in production in varying forms for over three decades, the Dennis Dart and variations that succeeded the original model would have to be one of the most successful types of bus ever to be built.

The first demonstrator was taken into stock during 1989, with the first production models entering service in 1990. The original bodywork being the Duple Dartline, this later being purchased by Carlyle who continued to build this model. Wrightbus of Ballymena was next to develop a body for the Dart, this being the Handybus which first appeared during 1991. In the same year, the Pointer came into existence, becoming the most popular model to feature on the Dart and Dart SLF chassis. Originally built by Reeve Burgess, the company was later purchased by Plaxton. Reeve Burgess had been part of the Plaxton Group from 1980, production later moving to Plaxton's Scarborough factory. These types became popular with London Buses Limited. A small quantity of the Northern Counties Paladin and East Lancs EL2000 body styles were taken into stock by operators for use on London contracts. Alexander introduced the Dash model in the early 1990s, with a number of these operating in London post-privatisation. Production of the Carlyle Dartline transferred to Marshall who continued to build a similar vehicle, although the step-entrance version was not taken up in large numbers. Two Wadham Stringer Portsdown saloons were also used in London, one being a demonstrator.

Volvo and MAN attempted to compete with the success of the Dart, Volvo with the B6, and MAN with a similar model. The B6 model was quite successful in the provinces. However, there was little take up in the London area.

The first low-floor Dart, the SLF, was first built in 1995, entering London service in 1996. This model became popular with London operators despite encountering some initial teething problems. A number of problems were met when planning to construct the low-floor model, the biggest being how to create a step free vehicle. Dennis overcame this by widening the chassis from 2.33m to 2.5m which allowed a standard wheelchair to fit just behind the front wheel arches of the vehicle. The size of the wheels was also reduced, allowing smaller wheel arches to be used.

Once the chassis had been successfully established, a number of body manufacturers designed models to fit the Dart SLF chassis. Plaxton altered the Pointer model, offering variants from 8.8m to 11.3m in length, the smallest being called the Mini Pointer Dart (MPD). Alexander introduced the ALX200, this also having big success in London, and like Plaxton they offered a variety of lengths. Marshall also experienced volume orders from London operators for their Capital model. Other manufacturers also offered products. MCV introduced the Evolution model which saw some success in London. East Lancs offered two variants, the Spryte and Myllennium models. UVG introduced the Urbanstar body, this later becoming the Caetano Compass. This latter model was replaced by the Nimbus and Slimbus models. Wright also introduced a new body style, this being the Crusader model, but this did not have the success of the Handybus.

The Dart SLF model in its true form was built by three different companies, firstly by Dennis which was amalgamated with Plaxton and Alexander to form Transbus in 2001, and lastly Alexander Dennis Limited (ADL) which took over from Transbus in May 2004. The Dart SLF was replaced during 2008 by the integral Enviro Dart, a model which had been built in unison with the Dart SLF since March 2006.

This book looks at the history of the Dennis Dart and Dart SLF in London. It is divided into several chapters, looking at each operator who has used the type.

David Beddall
Rushden, 2022

P41MLE was the first Dennis Dart SLF, being tested by London Buses Limited before being allocated to Centrewest at Uxbridge. In October 2003 it passed to F.E. Thorpe of Wembley for further London service. It is with this latter operator it is photographed. *Matthew Wharmby*

LONDON BUSES LIMITED

London Buses Limited was the first London area operator to take delivery of the Dennis Dart. Between 1989 and 1994 a large number of the type entered service carrying the Carlyle/Duple Dartline; Wrightbus Handybus; Reeve Burgess/Plaxton Pointer; East Lancs EL2000 and the Northern Counties Paladin, along with a Wadham Stringer Portsdown demonstrator.

A twenty-eight-seater Duple Dartline bodied Dennis Dart arrived at Catford in October 1989. The vehicle in question was registered G349CCK. A month later, it moved to Peckham for further use. It then moved around London Buses, being used by the company from a number of garages. A second demonstrator was also loaned to the company, this time registered G541JBV. This was a larger thirty-nine seat model measuring 9.0m in length. It was allocated to Stamford Hill but was not used in service. Dennis loaned a Dart chassis to London Buses at Fulwell during the early part of 1990, acting as a mechanical trainer.

The first twenty-seven production models arrived between March and April 1990. Fleet numbers DT1 to DT27 and registration marks G501-27VYE were allocated to these vehicles. The first eleven were allocated to Fulwell where they were used on routes R69 (Richmond-Hammersmith) and R70 (Richmond-Hampton Nurserylands). The others were allocated to Hounslow where they were used on the H21 (Hounslow circular), H22 (Richmond-Hounslow West Station) and H23 (Hounslow-Heathrow Cargo Terminal). Livery worn by these vehicles was all-red, relieved by a white waist-height band and a grey skirt. They were adorned with 'Harrier' branding.

DT28-57 were allocated to Selkent, these being registered G28-57TGW. They arrived between April and June 1990. DT28-41 were allocated to Orpington where they were used by Selkent on the low-cost Roundabout operation. They were put to use on the R1 (Bromley Common-Green Street Green-Orpington-Sidcup (Queen Mary's Hospital) and R11 (Green Street Green-Orpington-Sidcup). DT28 arrived early and was used as a type trainer. This vehicle was named *Pride of Carlyle* in June 1990. DT42-57 were allocated to Bromley where they were put to use on the 126 (Eltham-Beckenham Junction) and the 314 (Eltham Station-New Addington), the latter service being introduced in 1990 to replace the B1. They also saw service on the 336 and 396. They were taken into stock to replace Ford Transit minibuses, Leyland Nationals and Leyland Titans, the latter two types being reallocated within London Buses. In July, DT47 went on loan to Centrewest at Westbourne Park for a few days where it was put to use on the 31, a route that was later converted to Dennis Dart operation.

G541JBV was the second Duple Dartline bodied Dennis Dart demonstrator to be taken on loan by London Buses Limited, arriving in the latter part of 1989. It is captured by the camera in Chelmsford, after its stint in London. *David Moth*

DT58-70 (H458-70UGO) were allocated to South London when they arrived during August 1990. They were purchased to upgrade the 412 (Purley-West Croydon) to new rolling stock from 1 September. Most were originally stored at Norwood, with some being used as trainers at Thornton Heath, the home of this batch.

A solitary Portsdown bodied Dennis Dart was loaned from Wadham Stringer in August 1990, registered G895XPX. It was used in the Orpington area on the R1 and R11. It then moved on to Thornton Heath where it was not used in service. It moved to Westbourne Park in September where it operated the 28 and 31. After use there, it transferred to Barking and Walthamstow where, like Thornton Heath, it was not used. Willesden was the last garage it was used at, operating on route 206. It left London in November, passing to Southampton Citybus. No orders for this type were placed by London Buses.

Deliveries of the Carlyle Dartline continued with London United receiving the next batch, DT71-87. These vehicles were registered H71-4MOB, H575MOC, H76MOB, H577MOC, H78/9MOB, H880LOX, H81-7MOB. Arriving in September, they were allocated to Fulwell where they were used on the 285 between Kingston and Heathrow Airport, as well as being used on the R70 when required. The majority of the batch arrived in September, with DT81/3-6 being delivered during October. These also carried 'Harrier' branding.

The DT class put in an appearance in North London in September 1990 when Metroline received the first of a sizable batch of Darts. First to arrive were DT88 to DT94 (H588MOC, H89MOB, H890LOX, H91-4MOB). They were allocated to Willesden for use on the 206 between Kilburn Park and St Raphael's Estate. Metroline branded these vehicles as 'Skipper'.

Further DTs arrived with Metroline in November 1990 when H95-8MOB, H899LOX, H620MCM, H101-9MOB were allocated to Edgware. These vehicles followed on from

Selkent received the second batch of DT class Darts. Some were allocated to Orpington for use on the Roundabout network in that area. DT40 (G40TGW) is seen operating the R1 service, loading in Orpington town centre. *Ian Armstrong Collection*

the Willesden batch as DT95 to DT109. They displaced elderly BL class Bristol LH saloons from the 251 (Arnos Grove-Edgware-Stanmore Church) and MCW Metrobuses from the 288 (Edgware Station-Broadfields).

The last, but largest, batch of DT class Darts to be allocated to Metroline arrived between November and December 1990, taking up rolling stock numbers DT110-143 and DT156/7. They were registered H110MOB, H611MOM, H112-20MOB, H621MOM, H122-44MOB and H156/7MOB. North Wembley, an outstation of Harrow Weald, took delivery of this batch. They were used on the H15 (Harrow Weald-Harrow Weald Garage-Harrow Bus Station-Northwick Park Hospital) and H18 (Harrow Weald-Harrow Bus Station). DT124 to 143 were taken into stock to displace older SR class midibuses. Harrow Weald borrowed several of these vehicles on a daily basis for use on the H12 (Harrow Weald Garage-Northwick Park Station-Harrow Bus Station).

The gap in fleet numbers was filled by a small batch delivered to Hounslow in November. DT144-155 (H144-55MOB) were put to use on routes H24 (Hatton Cross Station-Feltham Station) and H25 (Butts Farm Estate-Hanworth-Feltham Station). The Darts operated these services alongside FR class and MR class midibuses.

Former demonstrator G349CCK arrived in November 1990. It was given fleet number DT168 and was initially put into store at Selkent's Catford garage before being allocated to Bromley in February 1991. In August it was re-registered 500CLT, retaining this registration mark until 1999.

The delivery of the remaining Carlyle Dartline bodied Darts did not take place until early 1991. Before their arrival, the first Wrightbus Handybus bodied Darts arrived in the Capital. London Buses Limited took delivery of a demonstration model in November 1990 registered JDZ2300. This vehicle was loaned from Wrightbus of Ballymena and operated on route 28 from Westbourne Park for the duration of its stay.

November also saw the arrival of the first Wrightbus Handybus production models with the Centrewest division. DW1 to DW14 arrived registered JDZ2301-14 and were allocated to Alperton. They took over operation on the 297 from December 1990.

These were followed by DW44 to DW58 (JDZ2344-58). Leaside Buses took delivery of this batch, allocating them to Wood Green. From this date they were used to replace MCW Metrobuses on route 84A.

At the same time, fourteen longer 9.0m Wrightbus Handybus bodied Darts were taken into stock. The classification code DWL was allocated to these vehicles to distinguish them from the shorter models. Rolling stock numbers DWL1 to DWL14 were allocated to these vehicles which carried registration marks JDZ2401 to JDZ2414 respectively. Seating thirty-five, they were allocated to the Westlink operation for use in the Kingston area on route 371.

The final batch of Carlyle Dartline saloons arrived between January and February 1991. DT158 to DT167 (H158-63, 264, 165-7NON) were allocated to London United who used them from Stamford Brook. The arrival of these Darts saw the displacement of Leyland Lynx saloons from the 283 (West Brompton-East Acton).

The batch of DT class Darts allocated to Bromley transferred west to Hounslow and Fulwell in May and June 1991. DT29, 41-54, 56/7, 168 were the vehicles that moved. They were used by their new garages on various single-deck duties, with those at Fulwell predominantly being used on the R68.

Further Wrightbus Handybus saloons began to arrive in February 1991, these being allocated to Centrewest at Westbourne Park. Delivery was split between February and March, with DW15-30 (JDZ2315-30) arriving first followed by DW31-43

January 1991 saw the arrival of fourteen longer DWL class Wright Handybus bodied Darts, this time with the Westlink operation. DWL5 (JDZ2405) represents the batch and is seen operating its intended route, the 371, stopped at the Richmond bus station stop. *Ian Armstrong Collection*

The mini and midibus operation operating from Centrewest's Westbourne Park garage were branded as Gold Arrow. February and March 1991 saw the arrival of DW15-43 for use on the 28 and 31. The major points of the routes operated can be seen displayed on the side of the DW21 (JDZ2321), which is seen loading in Camden Town. *Ian Armstrong Collection*

(JDZ2331-43). Seating twenty-six, they were used to displace the MA class Mercedes-Benz 811Ds on the 28 and 31, being given Gold Arrow fleet names. Shortly after arrival in March, DW36 was placed on loan with London General at Sutton. It was used for type training duties ahead of the delivery of Sutton's own batch of DWs. This batch stayed true to Westbourne Park until 1998 when they were replaced by new low-floor Dart SLFs.

Two additional batches of Wrightbus Handybus bodied Darts arrived in London during April. Seven of these were allocated to Selkent at Catford garage. These vehicles took up stock numbers DW59 to DW65 (JDZ2359 etc) and were put to use on the P4 (Brixton-Lewisham). However, DW59 was placed on loan to Selkent's Orpington garage from new where it was used on the R1 and R11.

Sutton received its own fleet of Darts in April, continuing the fleet numbering sequence as DW66-70 (H366-70XGC). The small batches gained Streetline branding and seated twenty-nine passengers.

A third body-style arrived in April 1991, this being the Reeve Burgess Pointer. The first nineteen arrived at London United's Hounslow garage in April and May. Registered H101-10THE, H611TKU, H112-9THE these vehicles introduced a new classification code to the London Buses Limited numbering system, the DR. Numbered DR1 to DR19, these vehicles were used on routes H37 and H91. In May, DR1 (H101THE) was sent on loan to Go-Ahead Northern, being used from Winlaton garage for a short period before returning to London. DR8 (H108THE) was a second vehicle to be placed on loan, this time a little closer to home. It was placed in the care of Metrobus

in July 1991 for examination. The arrival of DR1-19 at Hounslow caused DT148 to DT154 to move from Hounslow to Stamford Brook in August. DR15-9 transferred to Metroline's Cricklewood garage in February and March 1994.

A second batch of twelve Pointer bodied Darts also commenced delivery during April, and again delivery continued into May. DR20 to DR31 (H120-31THE) were allocated to South London at Streatham for use on the 249 (Crystal Palace-Tooting Bec Station). They remained at Streatham until this garage closed in March 1992, when they moved across to Norwood.

DR32-47 (H532-4, 835, 536-47XGK) followed in May and were allocated to London General's Merton garage. This batch also gained Streetline branding and were allocated to route 156. At the same time, five similar vehicles, DR48-52 (H548-52XGK), arrived at Stockwell for use on route 170.

Further Wrightbus Handybus bodied Darts flooded into London between May and July 1991. The former Handybus demonstrator JDZ2300 was formally acquired by London Buses Limited in May. It continued to operate from Westbourne Park garage and was allocated fleet number DW100.

A further fourteen Handybus Darts arrived in May numbered DW71 to DW84 (JDZ2371-84). Intended to operate with Centrewest from Westbourne Park, these vehicles went straight on loan to London United at Stamford Brook, returning to Centrewest in August. DW85-91 (JDZ2385-91) arrived in June, going straight to Westbourne Park. This was also the case with DW92 to DW99 (JDZ2392-9) and DW101 (KDZ5101) in September. Like the batch originally delivered to Centrewest, these

April and May 1991 saw the arrival of the first Pointer bodied Darts, at this time the Pointer being constructed by Reeve Burgess. Nineteen of the type, given the DR class code, were allocated to London United's Hounslow garage for routes H37 and H91. DR15 (H115THE) is seen on layover at Hounslow West Underground Station, this being the western terminus of the H91. *Ian Armstrong Collection*

London Central received the first of the long Plaxton Pointer bodied Dennis Dart DRL class in September 1991, when sixteen of the type were allocated to Peckham for use on the P11. DRL5 (J605XHL) is seen parked at Peckham garage, before heading back to Waterloo Station on the route. *Ian Armstrong Collection*

vehicles carried twenty-six seats. October saw the arrival of DW102-12 (KDZ5102-12) at Westbourne Park.

Westlink's DWL1 lost the standard fleet livery in September 1991 in favour of a white-based livery for Kingston Polytechnic. It was used on a contract for the Polytechnic.

Alongside the Wrightbus Handybus deliveries, a number of Pointer Darts also arrived in London. Three additional DRs were taken into stock by London United's Hounslow garage during August. J653-5XHL were purchased as top-up vehicles and were numbered DR53 to DR55.

Yet another class code was introduced in September 1991 when London Buses Limited took delivery of its first 9.0m long Pointer Darts. DRL1 to DRL16 (J601-16XHL) were allocated to London Central at Peckham and featured a seating capacity of thirty-four compared with twenty-eight of the DR class. They were put to use on local service P11 (Waterloo Station-Peckham) wearing a red livery complete with a grey skirt, and *Hoppa* branding.

Metroline's DT97/8, 100/2/4-7 moved from Edgware to North Wembley during October 1991.

November and December deliveries reverted to the shorter DR class Pointer Darts. London United were again the recipients of the type. The first pair were numbered DR56 and DR57 (J156/7GAT) and joined similar vehicles at Hounslow. They displaced Carlyle Dartline bodied Darts DT144 and DT155 to Stamford Brook in November, joining others which had transferred earlier in the year. DR58 to DR64 (J158-64GAT) were the final Dart deliveries of 1991. They were placed into store at Fulwell upon arrival in London during December, before being allocated to Hounslow for use on the H37.

January 1992 saw the arrival of DR65 to DR72 (J365-72GKH), these again being allocated to London United. Allocated to Hounslow, they replaced DR1-9 which transferred to Fulwell. They were joined there in February by DR73 to DR80 (J373-80GKH) and together operated route 290 (Twickenham-Staines), working alongside DT class Dennis Darts.

The first Pointer Darts to be allocated to Metroline arrived in February and March 1992. At this time eighteen DR class saloons entered service from Edgware. Like those allocated to Hounslow the previous year, the DRs were used to replace slightly older DT class Darts. At this time, DT95/6/9, 101/3/8/9 moved across to Willesden for further service. The new Darts were numbered DR81 to DR98 (J381GKH etc) and were used on services 143, 251, 288 and 303 respectively.

DT28 (G28TGW) and DT55 (G55TGW) lost their original registration marks in February 1992, being re-registered using former Routemaster registrations 49CLT and WLT575.

Twenty-two DR class Darts, DR99 to DR120, arrived with London United between March and May 1992, and were allocated to Shepherd's Bush, these being the first of their type to operate from this garage. The batch carried registration marks J599, 610, 101-10, 611, 112-20DUV. They were intended for Fulwell for the conversion of the 33 (Fulwell-Hammersmith). DR99-104 soon moved to Shepherd's Bush, the others staying at Fulwell.

DR112 (J112DUV) was placed on loan with the Eastern Counties Omnibus Company in May 1992. It was allocated to Norwich, where it was used on Park & Ride services for a week. It then moved on to Lincolnshire Road Car in June before officially being delivered to Fulwell in July.

Twenty-one DR class Darts followed in June which were again allocated to London United. Originally allocated to Fulwell, they soon joined the batch mentioned above at Wood Lane, an outstation of Shepherd's Bush which operated routes 9A, 72 and 220.

London United also received the first Dart deliveries of 1992, these arriving in January as DR65-80. The second part of the batch, DR73-80, was allocated to Fulwell for use on the 290. DR76 (J376GKH) is seen on this route, paused at Staines bus station. *Ian Armstrong Collection*

DR81-98 were the first Plaxton Pointer bodied Dennis Darts to be allocated to Metroline, all going to Edgware for routes 143, 251, 288 and 303. DR88 (J388GKH) is seen showing off its Skipper branding whilst on layover at Brent Cross Shopping Centre. *Ian Armstrong Collection*

These vehicles continued the numbering sequence from DR121 to DR141 (J121-41DUV) and arrived between April and June.

Delivered alongside the DR class Darts were fourteen Wrightbus Handybus bodied Dennis Darts. DW113 to DW116 (LDZ9113-6) arrived in April, followed by DW117-25 (LDZ9117-25) in May. The batch was complete in September when DW126 (LDZ9126) was taken into stock. All were allocated to Centrewest at Westbourne Park, from where they operated the 70.

Deliveries of the longer 9.0m Pointer Dart resumed in July and August 1992 when nine were taken into stock by Chalk Farm garage for route 46. Registrations K817-25NKH were carried by these vehicles, which were allocated fleet numbers DRL17-25. They were joined by twelve similar vehicles at Chalk Farm for the 274. They were numbered DRL26 to DRL37 (K826-8NKH, K429-37OKH).

Westlink's DWL2 joined sister DWL1 in an all-over livery for Kingston University, receiving this by September 1992.

Leaside Buses took delivery of their first Pointer bodied Darts in October 1992 when DRL38 to DRL52 (K538-52OKH) were received. They were allocated to Wood Green where they displaced older DW class Darts on route 84. DW44 and DW45 transferred to London General who allocated the pair to Sutton. DW46-51/3-7 were also reallocated to London General at Victoria Basement for further use. The final pair, DW52 and DW58, were placed under the care of Metroline who allocated them to Willesden.

At the same time London General received ten similar vehicles numbered DRL53 to DRL62 (K853LGN etc), followed by eleven more, DRL63 to DRL73 (K863-73LGN), in November. All twenty-one were allocated to Victoria Basement.

A number of London United's shorter DR class Darts were reallocated from Shepherd's Bush to the newly established Wood Lane outstation in October 1992. The vehicles concerned were DR72-4, 100-8.

Further 8.5m Plaxton Pointer bodied Dennis Darts arrived in London during November 1992. DR142 to DR148 (K242-8PAG) were allocated to Metroline's Edgware garage where they were used to displace MR class MetroRider midibuses to Cricklewood.

November also saw the arrival of similar length Darts at London General's Merton garage. DR149 to DR153 (K149-53LGO) were used on services 155 and 355, operating alongside DW class Darts.

The final Dart deliveries for 1992 arrived in December. These were in the form of six Handybus bodied Darts numbered DW127 to DW132 (K127-32LGO). They were allocated to London General and operated from Merton.

Several DWs were re-registered between December 1992 and January 1993. DW46 became WLT346; DW48 was re-registered WLT548 and DW52 to 352CLT. These were all done in December 1992. The final vehicle to be treated was DW45, which was given registration mark 545CLT in January 1993.

The final batch of Wrightbus Handybus bodied Darts were delivered in early 1993. The first nineteen, DW133 to DW151 (NDZ3133-51), arrived in February and were followed in March by DW152-170 (NDZ3152-70). Of these, DW133-160 were allocated to East London's Barking garage, with DW161-170 being added to North Street, Romford's allocation. The batch gained East London Hoppa branding. However, those allocated to Romford only lasted there until November 1993 when they transferred elsewhere within London Buses. DW160 and DW161 were reallocated to London General's Merton garage, whilst DW162 to DW170 were added to the large number of the type operating with the Centrewest division. They were allocated to Alperton where they were given Harlesden Challenger branding for use on the 297.

London Northern branded their Darts as Midilink. Over the summer of 1992, the Company took delivery of DRL17 to DRL36, which were shared between routes 46 and 274. DRL21 (K821NKH) is seen parked at Marble Arch before heading back to Camden Town on route 274. *Ian Armstrong Collection*

Those at Romford only lasted there until November 1993, after which time they moved across to London General or Centrewest. DW164 (NDZ3164) was one that moved to Centrewest, operating from Alperton garage. They were primarily transferred for use on the 297, being allocated Harlesden Challenger fleet names. DW164 is photographed showing off this branding at Golders Green, whilst operating a journey on the 226. *Ian Armstrong Collection*

A second batch of longer DWL class Wrightbus Handybus bodied Darts was delivered alongside the batch mentioned above. DWL15 to DWL26 (NDZ3015-26) arrived at Barking during February. Like the shorter versions, this batch was allocated East London Hoppa branding.

Another Carlyle Dartline bodied Dart was given a Routemaster registration mark in February 1993. At this time, DT32 (G32TGW) was re-registered VLT240.

London United's Hounslow garage took delivery of thirteen Plaxton Pointer bodied Darts in April 1993. Numbered DRL96 to DRL108, these vehicles were registered K96-8, 199, 210, 101-8SAG and were put to use on route H32. However, they could be found working any of Hounslow's midibus routes.

London General took delivery of the batch that numerically came before DRL96-108. DRL74 (K574MGT) was the first to arrive, putting in an appearance during April. The rest followed slowly, being delivered to London between May and July. They filled the gap in the numbering system, becoming DRL75 to DRL95 (K575MGT etc). Allocated to Victoria Basement, they were used on the 211 (Fulham Broadway-Hammersmith) and the 511 (Waterloo-Victoria) and carried Streetline branding. DRL76 was sent to Malaysia on behalf of Dennis Commercial Vehicles before arriving in London in August 1993.

The next thirty-eight DRL class Darts were also slow in being delivered. DRL109 to DRL146 (K109-33SRH, L136-146VRH) arrived between May and November 1993. They were ordered for use on East London services 300, 308, 309 and 325, but could

East London took delivery of twelve DWL class Wright Handybus bodied Dennis Dart saloons for use at Barking. DWL20 (NDZ3020) represents the batch which arrived in February 1993. They gained East London Hoppa branding as can be seen. The split-step entrance can also be seen in this view. *Ian Armstrong Collection*

also be found operating other single-deck services from their home garages. DRL109 to 117 were allocated to Upton Park, whilst Barking took delivery of DRL118 to DRL126. DRL121 went on loan to Upton Park for driver training duties. DRL127-35 were allocated to Stratford. North Street, Romford took delivery of three of the batch, these being DRL136 to DRL138 respectively. The final handful, DRL139-146, were all allocated to Upton Park.

A much smaller batch of twelve Pointer Darts arrived over the course of August and September 1993. DRL147 to DRL158 (L247, 148-58WAG) were allocated to the South London operation, being based at Norwood for use on the 322 (Crystal Palace-Vauxhall). Members of this small batch were placed on loan to other operators before entering service on their intended route. In August, DRL147 and DRL148 went on a 2-day loan to Capital Citybus where they were used on the 236. At the same time, DRL149-51 went on loan to London United's Hounslow garage where they were used on the 555, 556, 557 and 575, these returning to South London in December 1993. DRL153-8 were placed in store at Croydon until December, when they finally entered service on the 322.

Routes 555, 556, 557 and 575 received their own batch in December, allowing DRL149-51 to return to South London. DRL159-64 (L159-64XRH) entered service in January 1994. DRL163 was placed on a two-week loan in January 1994 with the Wycombe Bus Company.

DW47 (JDZ2347) was given registration mark WLT470 in January 1994, joining others of the type that had been re-registered the previous year.

DRL147 (L247WAG) was one of a batch delivered to South London during the summer of 1993. It is seen heading towards Elephant & Castle on route 322. *Collin Lloyd/Jeff Lloyd Collection*

London United received the final members of the DRL class in February 1994. DRL165 to DRL169 carried registration marks L165-9YAT, with the final pair, DRL170/1, being registered L170/1CKH. Hounslow was again chosen to house these vehicles.

Six Plaxton Pointer bodied Dennis Darts lost their original registrations in favour of cherished registration marks from withdrawn Routemasters. In January, DRL94 and DRL95 lost their registrations (K594/5MGT) in favour of WLT994 and WLT395 respectively. The next three re-registrations took place in July. DR11 (H611TKU) was allocated registration WLT931; DR111 (J611DUV) became WLT946, whilst DRL100 (K210SAG) was re-registered ALM2B. DR100 (J610DUV) joined these vehicles, becoming VLT23 in August 1994.

A small batch of 9.0m Dennis Dart saloons with East Lancs EL2000 bodywork was delivered to London Buses Limited in June 1994. These took up rolling stock numbers DEL1 to DEL11 and were registered L901-911JRN. London Central took delivery of these vehicles and allocated them to Camberwell. They were used on the 484 (Camberwell Green-Lewisham) and the P5 (Elephant & Castle-Clapham North Station).

At the same time, another new body style was introduced to London. Nineteen 9.0m Northern Counties Paladin bodied Dennis Darts were allocated to the London Northern operation at Holloway. They took fleet numbers DNL101-10/2-20 and were registered L101-10/2-20HHV. They were used to update the rolling stock on the C2, for which all but DNL118 and DNL119 carried route branding and Camden Link names. A livery of red with a white roof and grey skirt was worn by the batch, which was used to displace Optare StarRider midibuses.

Four DT class Darts were re-registered in August 1994. DT75 (H575MOC) became WLT329; DT77 lost its original registration H577MOC to become WLT339. DT80 (H880LOX) was re-registered 236CLT at this time. The final vehicle was DT164 (H164NON) which became WLT804.

Between September 1994 and January 1995, London Buses Limited sold its various divisions to private operators. The vehicles operated by them passed to these new companies. The large quantity of Dennis Darts was divided amongst these new operating concerns. Details of which vehicles went where can be found under the relevant operator later in this book.

London Northern received a batch of nineteen Northern Counties Paladin bodied Dennis Darts in 1994. They were used on the C2 for which they gained full route branding. This can be seen applied to DNL103 (L103HHV), which is seen with Camden Link branding. *Ian Armstrong Collection*

Eleven East Lancs EL2000 bodied Dennis Dart saloons were allocated to London Central's Camberwell garage for use on the 484 and P5 in June 1994. DEL3 (L903JRN) is seen on the 484, parked at Lewisham Bus Station. *Ian Armstrong Collection*

R&I TOURS

R&I Tours were the second operator to take delivery of the Dennis Dart in the London area. The company was successful in winning the tenders for London routes C11 and C12 in July 1990. For these services they purchased thirteen 9.0m Carlyle Dartline bodied Dennis Darts. These vehicles were registered G121-9RGT and G216-20LGK respectively. A smart livery of silver, blue and red was applied to these vehicles.

An additional Carlyle Dartline was acquired by R&I in 1990. Originating with the Isle of Man Transport as CMN-12A, it was re-registered RIB7002 by R&I joining the others on the C11 and C12. It was short lived in London, transferring to R&I's Milton Keynes operation. It was later numbered 232 by the company.

The second batch delivered for the C11 and C12 were registered in the G-LGK registration sequence. G216LGK is seen passing St Pancras blinded for its return journey to Archway on the C11. *Gary Seamarks*

A Plaxton Pointer bodied Dart was acquired in July 1922 carrying registration mark J823CGF, numbered 233. It was used on service T in the Docklands area. In December 1994, it was re-registered to 33LUG and was later used in the Milton Keynes area.

A more significant batch of 9.0m Pointer Darts arrived in March 1993 for use on route 268 (Golders Green Station-Finchley Road). The vehicles concerned were registered K414-9MGN. They were allotted rolling stock numbers 234 to 239.

R&I Tours won the contract for the 112 in 1994, for which additional Plaxton Pointer bodied Dennis Dart saloons were purchased. A pair of 9.0m long Darts, 240 and 241 (M498/9ALP), were first to arrive in August. They were joined by four longer 9.8m Pointer Darts registered M503-6ALP, which were numbered 245 to 248. As well as the 112, these vehicles could also be found operating the C11 and C12.

The operations and vehicles of R&I Tours were acquired by MTL London Northern on 24 October 1995. At this time, Darts 216, 219, 220/1/4, 232-42 and 245/8 transferred to their new owner.

R&I Tours won the contract for the 112 in 1994, purchasing six Plaxton Pointer bodied Darts to operate the service. 246 (M504ALP) is seen entering Brent Cross bus station having completed its journey in from Ealing. *Collin Lloyd/Jeff Lloyd Collection*

LONDON COUNTRY (NORTH WEST)

London Country (North West), under the ownership of Luton & District, was the third operator to take delivery of the Dennis Dart saloon. The company traditionally operated in the Slough, High Wycombe, Watford and Hemel Hempstead areas. They also had a couple of LRT contracts into the Harrow area of North London. On 19 January 1991, London County (North West) commenced operation of the 258 between Watford Junction and South Harrow. For this service, seven 8.9m long Carlyle Dartline bodied Dennis Darts were purchased. The batch was registered in two different registration series. DC1 to DC4 carried registration marks H922-6LOX, whilst DC5 to DC7 were registered H242-4MUK. The route was operated from Garston garage in Watford.

Like the R&I Tours Carlyle bodied Dennis Darts, those delivered to London Country (North West) were registered in two different series, H-LOX and H-MUK. DC4 (H926LOX) is seen on layover at Watford Junction Station. *Ian Armstrong Collection*

METROBUS

Over the years, Metrobus has taken stock of a large number of Dennis Dart and Dennis Dart SLF saloons for operations in both Greater London and Sussex.

The first Darts arrived in August 1991 when a batch of seven 8.5m Pointer Darts was purchased for use on the 146 (Bromley-Downe), which Metrobus had won from Crystals of Dartford. The vehicles concerned were registered J701-7EMX. They were also used on Metrobus' commercial service 351.

Nine longer 9.0m Pointer Darts arrived in November 1992. K708-16KGU were allocated fleet numbers 708 to 716 by Metrobus and were put to use on the 358 between Orpington, Bromley and Crystal Palace. By 1994, the 358 had grown in popularity and larger vehicles were required, as this batch was no longer suitable. L717-20OMV, measuring 9.8m, arrived in April 1994. M721-4GGO followed in December. The introduction of these new Darts caused the cascade of older Darts in the fleet. The K-registered Darts moved from the 358 to the 146 and 351, whilst the original J-plate Darts moved on to operate the 352. An increase in peak vehicle requirement (PVR) on the 358 during 1995 saw the addition of two Pointer Darts. N725 and 726KGF appeared during November.

K714KGU was originally purchased by Metrobus for the 358 between Orpington and Crystal Palace. The popularity of the route meant that these Darts proved to be too small, and a fleet of higher capacity Darts were purchased. It is seen operating route 138 to Coney Hall, just about to depart from the stop at Bromley North Station. *Ian Armstrong Collection*

In November and December 1995, J702/5EMX were loaned to Kentish Bus to allow this company to repaint a batch of Optare MetroRiders which had been acquired by Metrobus around this time.

The first low-floor Dart SLFs arrived with Metrobus in January 1998 numbered 741 to 745 (R741-5BMY). These Plaxton Pointer saloons measured 10.0m in length and were intended for the 233 (Swanley-Eltham), a route won from Kentish Bus. However, problems were encountered in the Sidcup area where the Dart SLFs were too big for the route. Therefore, they were reallocated to route 181 between Lewisham and Downham. Three additional Pointer Dart SLFs were added to complete the allocation on the 181. These were numbered 746-8 (R746-8FGX). The batch operated the 181 until it was lost to Stagecoach London in March 2001. After this they were reallocated within Metrobus, being renumbered 241-8 in August 2001.

A second batch of Plaxton Pointer bodied Dennis Dart SLFs arrived in January 1999. Registered P301-8HDP, these vehicles had originated with Limebourne Travel before being repossessed in 1998. They were numbered 301 to 308 by Metrobus. Four were allocated to Godstone, the other four to Green Street Green. Those allocated to the latter garage were used on the 352 (Bromley North-Lower Sydenham). The Godstone quartet moved to Orpington in 2000, remaining there until August 2003, when they moved south to Crawley.

A trio of 10.2m Alexander ALX200 bodied Dart SLFs were taken into stock during July 1999. 309 to 311 (T309-311SMV) were allocated to Lewes garage where they remained until that garage closed in July 2003. After this, they moved to Crawley

744 (R744BMY) is captured by the camera heading towards Lewisham on the 181 wearing the blue and yellow Metrobus livery. *Matthew Wharmby*

where they were put to use on the 100 Gatwick Direct service. In 2005, the two-tone blue livery was applied to the three saloons These were the only Alexander ALX200s to be purchased by the Company.

Between August 1999 and September 2000, twenty-one 8.8m Plaxton Pointer MPD bodied Dart SLFs were taken into stock by Metrobus for various uses. The first arrived at Godstone in August 1999 registered T312-6SMV. They were taken into stock to convert TfL service 146 (Bromley-Downe) and commercial service 246 (Bromley-Edenbridge) to the type. 339, 341-3 (W339/41-3VGX) were next to arrive in March 2000, again being allocated to Godstone for routes 464 (Tatsfield-Biggin Hill-New Addington) and 494 (Shirley-West Croydon). The next nine MPDs, 791-9, arrived in May 2000 registered W791-9VMV. They were put to use on country service 200 (Gatwick Airport-Crawley), for which they were given specific route branding. In August 2001, they were renumbered 291 to 299. 344 (X344YGU) was a solitary MPD taken into stock during August 2000 for use on local services in the Caterham area. 346 and 347 (X346/7YGU) completed the twenty-one MPDs when they arrived in September. They were used on route 56 between Lewes and Brighton, being allocated to Lewes. They passed to Brighton & Hove in July 2003 when Lewes closed.

Ten 10.7m Pointer bodied Dart SLFs were taken into stock in November 1999 for use on routes T33 (West Croydon-Addington Village) and 352 (Sydenham-Bromley North Station). 322 to 331 (V322-31KMY) arrived during this month. They were joined in April 2000 by 317/9, 332/4-9 and 341/2 which carried matching W-VGX registration marks. Before the T33 started in May 2000, some of the batch was used on the

310 (T310SMV) was one of only three Alexander ALX200 bodied Dart SLFs to be purchased by Metrobus. It is seen wearing the 'country' livery whilst loading in Crawley bus station. *Matthew Wharmby*

Gatwick Airport provides the backdrop to a pair of MPDs purchased by Metrobus in 2001 for route 200. W799VMV is the front vehicle and can be seen carrying branding for the service. *Collin Lloyd/ Jeff Lloyd Collection*

temporary service TL1. A handful started life at Godstone, before all being allocated to Green Street Green. In May 2002, the T33 and 359 were allocated to Godstone, with ten of the batch moving with the route.

Nine Pointer MPDs for use on the 367 (Bromley North-West Croydon) arrived in March 2001. They were numbered 348/9, 351-4/6-8 (Y348HMY etc). Speed bumps along the route caused problems for them, which meant these vehicles were temporarily used on the 233 between Eltham and Swanley.

Two batches of second-hand step-entrance Darts were acquired in March 2001. The first eight carried Marshall bodywork, arriving from the City of Oxford Motors. Rolling stock numbers 762 to 769 were allocated to the batch which carried registration marks M502, 511, 516, 520, 506-8, 518VJO. They were initially used on services in the Crawley area before being replaced by new rolling stock in 2004. After this time, they were put to further use as driver training vehicles, when they were renumbered 7762-9. The first four were allocated to Orpington, the others to Crawley. The second batch arrived from Brighton & Hove. These forty-seaters were numbered 783/6/7 and carried registration marks J983/6/7JNJ. The trio carried Plaxton Pointer bodywork.

Metrobus hired three Marshall bodied Dennis Dart SLFs in April 2001 from Dawson Rentals. The first pair were registered P830/1BUD and were used from Crawley until July. S719KNV also arrived at the same time and was allocated to Godstone. It also returned to Dawson Rentals in July 2001. For the duration of their stay, they took up fleet numbers 397 to 399.

381-9, 391-3 (Y381-9, 391-3HKE) arrived in July and August 2001, allocated to Orpington. These were ordered for use on routes 233, 336, 367 and 494. It was intended that some of these vehicles were to be used on the 138 but due to problems on the Downham estate, the batch was delayed in entering service on this route.

May 2002 saw additional vehicles required for the 358, the gap being filled by the acquisition of four 10.0m Pointer Darts from London Central. The former LDP24 to

Route T33 gained a batch of Plaxton Pointer 2 bodied Dennis Dart SLF saloons in November 1999, sharing them with the 352. 325 (V325KMY) is seen entering Addington Village Bus Station in the 100% red livery applied to the batch. *Liam Farrer-Beddall*

These were followed in April by another new body style. At this time eighteen Caetano Nimbus bodied Dart SLFs were purchased for use on town services in the Redhill area after Arriva Southern Counties pulled out of that area. They were numbered 359, 361-9, 371-4 (Y359HMY etc). These were the longest Dart SLFs that had been operated by Metrobus, measuring 11m. 359, 361-3, 377-9 arrived slightly later, appearing in July 2001. 362 (Y362HMY) is seen at Redhill Bus Station sporting the new two-tone blue livery introduced by Metrobus for the Crawley operation. *Liam Farrer-Beddall*

The summer of 2001 saw the arrival of twelve Plaxton Pointer MPD bodied Dennis Dart SLF saloons, which were shared between several routes. 388 (Y388HKE) is seen parked at Eltham Station whilst operating the 233. *Ian Armstrong Collection*

LDP27 (P724-7RYL) were taken into stock at this time, being numbered 224 to 227 by Metrobus. In January 2004, they were no longer needed and were sent to Crawley for further use. London General provided three similar vehicles in June 2002 to fill the void on route 352. LDP11, 113 and 114 (WLT311, S113/4EGK) were loaned from the latter operator, taking fleet numbers 211, 213 and 214 for the duration of their stay with Metrobus.

In December 2002, Kent County Council purchased a solitary vehicle registered GJ52HDZ. It was used on contracted service 401 between Tunbridge Wells and Westerham/Chartwell, and the 421 between Swanley and Sevenoaks. Initially allocated to Southlands Coaches, it was allocated to Metrobus in May 2004 who put it to use from Godstone. It remained with Metrobus until April 2006 when it returned to Kent County Council.

Two Pointer bodied Dart SLFs were delivered in March 2003. At this time, 320 and 321 (LX03OJP and OJN) were delivered to Crawley, remaining in store until May. They were used on the 526, gaining route branding in November 2003. In March 2008, route branding for the 200 was applied to the vehicles.

Nineteen 10.7m Pointer Dart SLFs followed in August for use on various TfL contracts in South London. The batch took up fleet numbers 201-19, registered SN03WKU/Y, WLA/E/F/H/L/P/U/X/Z, WMC/F/G/K/P/T/V/Y. The first five, 201-205, were allocated to Godstone for use on the 246 (Bromley North-Westerham). In February 2006, Godstone closed and the batch moved to Metrobus' new garage in Croydon. At the end of the year, the 246 was lost, the batch was then refurbished and reallocated to Crawley for use on town route 2. The next eight, 206 -213, were allocated to Crawley for use on TfL service 405 (West Croydon-Redhill). In April 2005, the route and vehicles moved to Godstone, only to move to Green Street Green and Croydon in

February 2006. In June 2007, 208 and 209 were converted to driver training vehicles, being renumbered 7208/9. The final six members of the batch were allocated to Green Street Green for use on the 130 (New Addington-Norwood Junction).

August 2003 also saw the arrival of another nineteen Pointer MPDs at Green Street Green. They took up rolling stock numbers 271 to 289 (SN03YBA/B/C/G/H/K/R/S/T/X/Y/Z, YCD/E/F/K/L/M/T).

251 to 256 (SN54GPV/X/Y/Z, GRF/K) were further 8.8m MPDs allocated to Green Street Green. They arrived in December 2004. They were used to replace the final step-entrance Dennis Darts on TfL services.

The Dartford operations of Tellings-Golden Miller were acquired by Metrobus in March 2005. With this came four Caetano Nimbus bodied Transbus Darts which were being used on the R2 in Orpington. These vehicles were numbered 220 to 223, registered KX04HRD/E/F/G. These were shorter than the Caetano Nimbus saloons already in operation in the Redhill area, measuring 10.5m. They remained in use with Metrobus until May 2007 when they were returned off lease.

The penultimate batch of Darts to be purchased by Metrobus arrived in April and May 2006. Twelve East Lancs Esteem bodied ADL Darts were taken into stock at this time numbered 257 to 268 (PN06UYL/M/O/P/R/S/T/U/V/W/X/Y). Allocated to Croydon they were used on routes 138 and 367. They were joined by a batch of nine similar vehicles in September 2006. At this time 228-236 (PO56JEU, JFA/E/F/G/J/K/N/U) entered service on the 146 and 336. Both batches measured 9.0m in length.

Addington Village finds 215 (SN03WMK), heading towards nearby New Addington on route 130. The lines for the Croydon Tramlink can be seen on the left of the photograph. *Liam Farrer-Beddall*

223 (KX04HRG) represents the four Caetano Nimbus bodied Dart SLFs taken into stock from Tellings-Golden Miller in March 2005. The last member of the batch, 223 (KX04HRG), is seen in Orpington operating route R2 to Petts Wood Station. *Jeff Lloyd Collection*

The final two batches of new Darts arrived in 2006 and carried the East Lancs Esteem body style. The first twelve were used mainly on the 138 and 367, and it is the latter route that 260 (PN06UYP) is seen operating when captured by the camera in Bromley town centre. *Liam Farrer-Beddall*

These were, however, not the last Dennis Dart SLFs to be acquired by the Company. In December 2007, the Orpington operations of First London were acquired by Metrobus. This saw thirty-five Marshall Capital bodied Dennis Dart SLFs enter the fleet, twenty-eight 8.9m versions and seven longer 10.2m saloons. The shorter Dart SLFs were numbered 120 to 147 (V360/1, 355/8DLH, LN51DVA-C/F, RZZ, SBO/U/V, LT02ZDA/C-G/M-P/R/S/U-X). 120 to 123 were the oldest, dating back to 1999, and these were soon sold, the rest being given an all-red repaint. Some were undergoing refurbishment at the time of takeover. The majority of these had left London by the end of 2008, with a handful hanging on until 2012/3. The seven longer Dart SLFs were numbered 380 to 386 (LK51JYJ/L/N, W359/61/73/4VLN). They were initially used on routes in Orpington and they were soon found operating on any of Orpington's routes. Three were later converted to driver training vehicles, the others being sold. The last three were allocated to Croydon for use on the 130. The remaining six were sold in January 2010.

Metrobus expanded further in October 2009 when they acquired the Horsham garage of Arriva Southern Counties. Alongside a batch of six Enviro 200s used on the 465, twelve Plaxton Pointer bodied Dennis Dart SLFs were also acquired. These were numbered 388 to 399 (P268FPK, P179LKL, P380, 281-3, 274, 285FPK, N232TPK, P278, 269FPK). 389 had been acquired by Arriva for use as a spare vehicle on the 465, and therefore wore a red livery. The others wore the corporate Arriva livery. They were soon transferred to Crawley for inspection, shortly after which 390, 393-6 and 398 were placed into service, the others being sold.

Three LDPs were borrowed from the main Go-Ahead London fleets in 2014. First to arrive was LDP192 (SN51UAE), taken on loan in January 2014 at Croydon. In April, LDP193, 200 and 207 were loaned to Green Street Green for use on Orpington area routes R2 and R9. At this time, the fleet operating Transport for London contracts were transferred to the main Go-Ahead London operation, retaining the Metrobus name.

Twenty-eight 8.9m long Marshall Capital bodied Dennis Dart SLF saloons were inherited from First London when they decided to sell their Orpington area operations to Metrobus in December 2007. 137 (LT02ZDG) is seen heading towards Chelsfield Village on route R3 shortly after departing Orpington Station. *Liam Farrer-Beddall*

COUNTY BUS

County Bus & Coach was formed when London Country (North East) company was divided into two separate companies. Traditionally the company operated in the Essex area but were successful in winning several contracts in East London.

Thirteen Plaxton Pointer bodied Dennis Darts arrived in October and November 1991 numbered DP301-313 (J301-13WHJ). They were put to use on newly won London routes W16 (Chingford Mount to Leytonstone Station) and 444 (Chingford Station to Edmonton). Measuring 9.0m in length, they had the ability to seat thirty-five. Edmonton garage was the base for these vehicles.

A handful of Wrightbus Handybus bodied Dennis Darts were also purchased by County Bus during 1992, four of which were allocated to the London operation. DW315 (J315XVX) was the first to arrive, being allocated to Edmonton on a temporary basis, from where it was used on the 444. For this use it was down-seated from forty to thirty-five seats, later being restored to its original capacity. DW316 and DW317 (J316/7XVX) soon followed but were allocated to Grays. All three were new to the Company in February 1992. DW314 (J314XVX) joined the trio during April 1992.

Six Pointer Darts arrived with County Bus in September 1992. The penultimate member of the batch, DP322 (K322CVX), is seen heading towards Harold Hill on the route 256. The Thameside fleet names can be seen on the side and front of the vehicle. *Collin Lloyd/Jeff Lloyd*

The final batch of Dennis Darts to join County Buses London operations comprised six Plaxton Pointer bodied vehicles, arriving in September 1992. At this time DP318 to DP323 (K318-23CVX) were taken into stock. They replaced a fleet of Mercedes-Benz minibuses that were being used by the Company on the 256. These vehicles were allocated to Grays.

County Bus took delivery of sixteen 10.0m long Plaxton Pointer bodied Dennis Dart SLFs in November 1997 for the take up of route 34 (Walthamstow Central-Barnet Church). These vehicles took up rolling stock numbers DPP416 to DPP431 and were registered R416-31COO.

Arriva took the decision to re-organise its operations in both London and the Home Counties, with changes taking effect from October 1998. Under these changes, County Bus, which by this time had become known as Arriva East Herts & Essex, lost its Edmonton garage, this being placed under the control of Arriva London North. No less then forty-seven buses and coaches were transferred to Arriva London from this date. This included DP301-313, DPP416-431 and DW314/5.

Route 34 gained sixteen low-floor Plaxton Pointer bodied Dennis Dart SLF saloons in 1997, these being branded as Lea Valley. DPP429 (R429COO) is seen at the Barnet terminus. *Ian Armstrong Collection*

TRANSCITY

Sidcup-based Transcity operated a small fleet of Plaxton Pointer bodied Dennis Darts in South-East London. The company took over the contract for the 286 (Greenwich-Eltham) from London Buses Limited in July 1992. For this, nine of the vehicles mentioned above were taken into stock by the company. Registration marks J220/1/3-9UGY were originally carried by these vehicles, later being reregistered J-HGY with the same numbers. They wore an all-green livery, relieved only by a yellow line and fleet names. The operation was short lived, with Kentish Bus taking over the operation and vehicles in October 1993.

Transcity operated a fleet of Plaxton Pointer bodied Dennis Dart saloons on the 286 service. J225HGY is seen passing through Well Hall Road, Eltham wearing their all-green livery, relieved only by the yellow fleet names. *Jeff Lloyd Collection*

THAMESWAY

Thamesway was formed in 1990 when the southern area garages of Eastern National were placed under the control of this new company. Prior to this, the company had been known as Eastern National. The latter company had been operating several LRT services since deregulation, being one of the first operators to win tenders for London routes. In 1992, Thamesway won the tender for the 214 (Parliament Hill Fields-Liverpool Street). For this service, the company purchased seventeen Plaxton Pointer bodied Dennis Darts. Allotted rolling stock numbers 901 to 917, they carried matching K-CVW registration marks. They wore the brown and mustard yellow livery and carried large badger logos on the sides. Thamesway's Ponders End garage took delivery of these vehicles.

903 (K903CVW) is seen passing St Pancras Station whilst heading towards Liverpool Street Station, wearing the new yellow and pink livery. *David Moth*

852 (N852CPU) shows off the red and yellow Mobility Bus livery applied to the four Marshall bodied Dennis Darts used by Thamesway on such services in the Romford area. It is captured by the camera in Romford town centre.
Matthew Wharmby

Further Darts arrived in October 1995 carrying Marshall C36 bodies. Numbered 851 to 854 (N851-4CPU), they were employed on the group of Mobility services in the Romford area. The quartet wore a red based livery with a deep yellow band.

Thamesway took delivery of new Pointer Darts for its non-London operations in Essex in 1995. Two of these were diverted to the London operations for use on the 307, Ponders End again being the recipient. The pair were numbered 944 and 945 (N944/5CPU) and replaced Leyland Olympian 4006 which suffered fire damage.

The brown and yellow livery eventually gave way to a yellow with pink sashes. The batch mentioned above could also be found operating routes 307 and W13 on occasions.

Thamesway lost the 214 in January 1998 to MTL London Northern. It was at this point that the Darts went on loan to MTL for continued operation of the 214. After this loan ceased, six of the batch went to First Capital, the others moving on to First Eastern Counties.

GREY GREEN

Grey Green took delivery of eight 9.0m Plaxton Pointer bodied Dennis Darts in August 1993. 934 to 941 (L934-941GYL) arrived to take over route 173 (Goodmayes-East Beckton). They were allocated to the company's Barking garage and wore the distinctive grey and green with orange stripe livery.

Two Plaxton Pointer bodied Darts were ready for use in the Strood area of Kent from April 1995. 950 and 951 (M950/1LYR) were used there until London Coaches took over services in that area. They then moved to Barking after a short period of loan at Maidstone.

The first low-floor Dart SLFs entered the fleet in early 1997. These came in the form of seventeen Alexander ALX200 bodied Dennis Dart SLFs measuring 10.25m in length. Numbered 952 to 968 (P952-68RUL), they were put to use on routes 20 (Walthamstow Central-Debden) and 167 (Ilford High Road-Debden Station). The batch was also used on Sundays on routes 173 and the 275 (Walthamstow Central and Claybury Broadway). These vehicles operated from Grey Green's Barking garage and wore the distinctive grey livery with green skirt and orange and white bands.

Grey Green took delivery of eight Plaxton Pointer bodied Dennis Dart saloons in August 1993 to operate route 173. 938 (L938GYL) is seen operating a journey on the 275, a route normally operated by low-floor buses. *Ian Armstrong Collection*

In November 1997, the Cowie Group was rebranded as Arriva, with Grey Green becoming known as Arriva London North East. Further details of the above vehicles can be found under the Arriva London heading.

In August 1997 Grey Green took over route 66 from County Bus. Some of the Alexander ALX200 bodied Dennis Dart SLFs, new to the company for routes 20 and 173, were used on this route. 959 (P959RUL) is seen on layover at Leytonstone Station. *Ian Armstrong*

WESTLINK

Westlink was the first of the London Buses Limited subsidiaries to be sold to a private company. West Midlands Travel acquired the company along with a batch of fourteen DWL class Wrightbus Handybus bodied Dennis Darts (DWL1-14) in January 1994. A livery of red with a blue and white stripe was introduced to the fleet. However, operation under West Midlands Travel control lasted for just over a year and a half, when, on the 15 September 1995, ownership passed to London United. The history of DWL1-14 after this date can be found under the London United heading.

Westlink took delivery of fourteen Wright Handybus bodied Dennis Dart saloons from London Buses Ltd in January 1994. A blue and white stripe was applied to the side of the vehicle as seen above. DWL6 (JDZ2406) is seen in Kingston town centre operating route K3, heading towards Esher. *Ian Armstrong Collection*

CENTREWEST/FIRST LONDON

Centrewest was the second of London Buses Limited's divisions to be sold, this time to the Company's management. The sale took place on 2 September 1994. Centrewest purchased London Buslines on 20 March 1996. Therefore, the fleet of Darts and Dart SLFs purchased by London Buslines are included under this heading.

Centrewest inherited the majority of the Wrightbus Handybus bodied Dennis Darts at privatisation, with no other variants being taken into stock. DW1-43, 72-126 and 162-170 were all transferred to the new company. DW162-8 operated from Alperton whilst the remainder operated from Westbourne Park. During their time with Centrewest, very little of interest took place regarding these vehicles. However, in November and December 1995, three DWs (17, 22 and 43) were loaned to Centrewest's Swanley garage for use on services in the Orpington area. They covered for the late arrival of new rolling stock and returned home to Westbourne Park in January 1996.

Thirty-nine 9.0m long Plaxton Pointer bodied Dennis Dart saloons were the first new single-decks to enter the Centrewest fleet. Routes 297 (Willesden-Ealing Broadway), and Orpington area services R1 and R11 were the recipients of these vehicles. Alperton received the first batch for route 297, these appearing in September and October 1995. DP18 to DP24 (N818-24FLW) were first to arrive, followed by DP25-32 (N825-32FLW). The other seventeen members of the batch, DP1-17 (N801-17FLW), were intended for Swanley garage. They were delivered to Centrewest during November for use in the Orpington area. These were given Orpington Buses fleet names, and both batches wore an all-over red livery relieved by a grey skirt. During 1996, routes R9 and 336 were also added to Orpington's route portfolio. At this time, Centrewest's operations in the area moved from Swanley to a new facility in St Mary Cray.

Further Pointer Darts were added to the Centrewest fleet in July 1996. D33 to D37 (N633-7ACF) were allocated to Uxbridge, where they naturally got Uxbridge Buses fleet names. These five Darts were intended for sister company London Buslines but were diverted to Centrewest. D33 lost its original registration (N633ACF) in November 1996 in favour of cherished registration 133CLT.

At the same time, four similar vehicles were delivered for use in the Orpington area. Numbered DP38 to DP41 (P408-11MLA), this quartet were used on the R9 service.

London Buslines, acquired by Centrewest on 20 March 1996 and retained as a separate business for a number of years, was successful in winning the tenders for

London routes 258, A10, C10, 331 and 285 during 1996, for which a number of vehicles were acquired. Two of these routes, plus the 203 (Hounslow-Staines), are relevant to the subject of this book. 601-610 (N601-10XJM) were taken into stock during January 1996 for use on the 258 (Watford Junction-South Harrow), measuring 9.8m. The route was officially transferred to First Centrewest on 23 January 1999. The Darts continued plying this route until low-floor Dennis Tridents took over in January 2001. Sixteen Pointer Darts followed in June 1996 for route 285 (Kingston-Heathrow Airport). They continued on from the 258 batch as 611-626 (N611-26XJM). A month later, the final step-entrance Darts for London Buslines arrived, again carrying Plaxton Pointer bodywork. Rolling stock numbers 627 to 632 were allocated to these vehicles which carried registration marks P627-32GCM. They were used on the 203 between Hounslow and Staines.

Capital Citybus was sold to First Group on 8 July 1998, joining Centrewest and London Buslines under First ownership. Capital Citybus themselves never purchased any new Wrightbus Handybus bodied Darts. A small number of the type were added to this operation in July 1998 for use on routes W6, W10, 299 and 357 in East London. Seven of the type, DW39-43 (JDZ2339-43) and DW72/3 (JDZ2372/3), transferred to Northumberland Park from Centrewest. These were the first vehicles in the fleet to receive the new red and yellow livery. Their new owners renumbered them to 639-645.

Two Dennis Darts were placed on loan to other First companies as 1998 drew to a close. Firstly, in October, DW75 was loaned internally to London Buslines for a short period. The second vehicle, D34 (N634ACF), went further afield to Cornwall. It was loaned to Western National, who operated the vehicle from its Cambourne garage.

Six Plaxton Pointer bodied Dennis Darts arrived in November from fellow First Group operator Thamesway. 691 to 696 (K901-6CVW) were taken into stock to operate

Seventeen Plaxton Pointer bodied Dennis Darts, DP1-17, were allocated to Centrewest's Swanley garage for use on the former Roundabout services in the Orpington area. The batch was intended for the R1 and R11 but could be found on any of the garage's Dart routes. DP7 (N807FLW) is seen at Orpington Station on route R3. *Ian Armstrong Collection*

The opening months of 1996 saw London Buslines, a subsidiary of Centrewest, take twenty-six Plaxton Pointer bodied Dennis Dart saloons into stock. They were used on the 258 and 285. 604 (N604XJM) is seen showing off the distinctive London Buslines livery whilst on layover in Watford. *Ian Armstrong Collection*

a rail replacement service for the Docklands Light Railway for which they wore a special blue and red livery.

The 297 was lost to Metroline in December 1998. The loss of the route led to the transfer of DP18-32 to First Beeline, operating in the Slough area.

The first low-floor Dennis Dart SLF arrived with Centrewest in August 1996. Plaxton Pointer bodied P41MLE was built in 1995 and was put through a number of trials by London Buses before being allocated to Centrewest. It was allocated to Uxbridge where it was used on the 222, operating alongside the first generation low-floor Dennis Lance SLFs. It remained with Centrewest until March 1999 when it passed to F.E. Thorpe of Wembley.

At the same time, seven similar vehicles arrived at Uxbridge numbered L1 to L7. Registered P401-7MLA, these vehicles were purchased for use on a new service between Uxbridge and Heathrow Airport. The A10 was supported by the British Airport Authority (BAA), and the batch wore a dedicated blue and yellow livery. The main aim of the route was to connect the termini with a new business area that was developing north of Heathrow. L7 was a spare vehicle for the route, and after the introduction of Marshall Capital bodied Dart SLFs at Uxbridge during 1997 L7 transferred to London Buslines in July.

London & Country was successful in winning the tender for the 105 (Heathrow Central-Greenford) in April 1996 at the expense of Centrewest. However, by November 1996 the 105 returned to Centrewest after the new operator found it difficult to operate the service. London & Country had established an outstation in Greenford in order to operate the 105. The batch of new Pointer bodied Dart SLFs purchased by the latter operator was also taken on loan by Centrewest. DSL25-36 (N225-36TPK) were renumbered L225-36 whilst under Centrewest ownership. They were reallocated to Alperton where they remained operating in a green livery until September 1997, after

Former Thamesway K906CVW is seen wearing the dedicated Docklands Light Railway livery whilst operating a rail replacement service for part of the line. *Matthew Wharmby*

The first batch of low-floor Dennis Dart SLFs arrived in August 1996 for the A10 service between Uxbridge and Heathrow Airport. The batch sported a special blue and yellow livery. This smart livery is being shown off by L4 (P404MLA), seen off route at Ruislip Station having worked a journey on the U1. *Ian Armstrong Collection*

which date they moved on to London Buslines at Southall. However, by February 1998 London & Country took the fleet of Dart SLFs back into ownership.

Alongside the Pointer Darts, a handful of DS class Darts were also used on the 105. In March 1997 they were displaced by three new Plaxton Pointer bodied Dennis Dart SLFs numbered L237 to L239. Registered P237-9NLW, these saloons were also allocated to Alperton. They received the green livery, similar to that worn by the former London & Country saloons. These also moved to London Buslines in September 1997.

May 1997 saw the arrival of the first of a large number of Marshall Capital bodied Dennis Dart SLFs to be purchased by Centrewest and First London. Forty-one 8.9m long Marshall Capital bodied Dart SLFs were allocated to Greenford to operate routes in the Ealing area, carrying Ealing Buses branding. They worked alongside a batch of Marshall Minibuses. The Darts were put to use on routes E3 (Greenford-Chiswick), E7 (Ealing Broadway-Ruislip) and E9 (Ealing Broadway-Yeading). Fleet numbers DM117 to DM157 were allocated to the batch which carried registration marks P117-46NLW, P247OEW, P148-57NLW. They were used to replace RW class minibuses on the routes mentioned above.

Route 90 in West London was split into two during August 1997, becoming the 90 and 490. London Buslines retained the 490 (Richmond Station-Hatton Cross), for which nine 10.2m long Marshall bodied Dart SLFs were ordered. These arrived numbered DML633 to DML641 and wore the yellow, red and maroon livery of London Buslines. Allocated to Southall, these saloons were registered R633/4, 835, 636-41VLX.

DML642 to DML653 were taken into stock by London Buslines during February 1998 to replace the London & Country Pointer Darts on the 105. Registration marks R642-653TLM were carried by these vehicles. 653 arrived earlier than the others, putting in an appearance in December 1997. Route branding was applied to a number of these vehicles.

P237NLW was the first of three new Pointer Dart SLFs purchased for the 105, working alongside a fleet of similar hired vehicles. They wore a similar livery and carried route branding as can be seen above. *Collin Lloyd/Jeff Lloyd Collection*

The Marshall Capital body style became synonymous with First London. The first forty-one of the type arrived in May 1997, replacing older midibuses on Ealing and Greenford area services, operating from Greenford garage. DM145 (P145NLW) represents this batch, seen at the Ealing Broadway terminus of route E7. Routes E3 and E9 also benefitted from this first batch of Dart SLFs. *Ian Armstrong Collection*

August 1997 saw the arrival of a small batch of Marshall Capital bodied Dennis Dart SLF saloons with the London Buslines operation. DML633-41 arrived for use on the 90 and 490. DML640 (R640VLX) is captured by the camera in Kew Road, Richmond whilst operating route 490. *Ian Armstrong Collection*

A third batch of fourteen 10.2m long Marshall Capital bodied Dart SLFs arrived between December 1997 and January 1998, this time to take up service on the 282 (Ealing Hospital-Greenford-Mount Vernon Hospital). Allotted rolling stock numbers DML165 to DML178 (R165-78TLM), they were built to single-door layout.

A batch of similar length Dart SLFs followed in March and was given numbers DML179-81 (R179-81TLM). They were followed in April by DML182-190 (R182-90TLM). Collectively the batch took up service from Uxbridge on the U4 (Uxbridge Station-Hayes).

A batch of shorter 9.4m DM class Dart SLFs also arrived in April. Numbered DM158 to DM164 (R158-64TLM), they were allocated to Greenford for use on the 195 (Charville Lane Estate-Ealing Hospital).

A larger intake of DM class Dart SLFs arrived during April and May 1998. Thirty-four of the type were allocated to Westbourne Park to replace the aging fleet of Wrightbus Handybus bodied Darts inherited from London Buses Limited. Numbered DM201-234 (R201-34TLM) they carried the Gold Arrow fleet name, although this was more discreet than on their predecessors. This batch was ordered to replace the DWs on route 31 (Chelsea-Camden Town). DM201-228 remained in use until 2004/2005 when they were cascaded to First Glasgow. DM229-234 moved across to Hackney Wick at this time.

Further deliveries of the 10.2m variant at Uxbridge took place in June. It was at this time that six of the batch, DML191 to DML196 (R191-6VLD), arrived with First London. The remaining four did not arrive until September, at which time they took up registration marks S197-9, 220KLM, and continued the numbering sequence on as DML197 to DML200.

At the same time, four similar length DML class Dart SLFs arrived at Westbourne Park. DML249 to DML252 (R677-80MEW) were acquired for use on a special service between Paddington Station and various hotels in the Marylebone and Marble Arch areas. Painted silver, these vehicles connected the hotels with Heathrow Express trains from Paddington. The batch were given registration marks 809-11DYE and 292CLT in July 1998. The service was short-lived, lasting until September 1999, after which time the batch reverted to its original registration marks and moved on to Bristol Airport, which at the time was owned by First Group.

The final deliveries for 1998 arrived in December in the form of eighteen dual-door DML class Dart SLFs. DML235-48, 253-6 (S235-48KLM, S253-6JLP) were allocated to Alperton from where they were used on route 92 (St Raphael's Estate-Ealing Hospital). The 92 gained a fleet of double-decks in 2004, with this batch being transferred to Uxbridge where they remained until 2009.

The intake of new Dart SLFs for 1999 commenced in March. At this time, seven shorter 8.9m saloons arrived and introduced a new class code to First London, the DMS. DMS257 to DMS263 (T257-63JLD) were purchased to replace the ill-fated Marshall ML integral minibuses at Greenford. They later moved around the First London operation as and where they were required, lasting until 2011 when they were withdrawn.

The next batch to arrive did so in May and June. Forty-three DMs were allocated to Westbourne Park, converting routes 28 and 328 to low-floor Darts. The short Dart SLFs were required for this service due to the narrow streets on the route. These routes, along with the 31, were double-decked in 2004, after which time this batch of Dart SLFs moved to Alperton, displacing similar single-doored Darts. This batch took up rolling stock numbers DM264 to DM306 (T264-99, 430, 301-6JLD).

Westbourne Park operated four Dart SLFs in a silver livery for a short period of time for use on a service connecting hotels in the Marble Arch area with Heathrow Express trains at Paddington. DML251 (811DYE) is seen loading at Paddington Station wearing this livery. *Collin Lloyd/Jeff Lloyd Collection*

A solitary Marshall Dart, DML336 (T336ALR), was allocated to Uxbridge in August, built to single-door layout to match the batch already in operation from this garage. It remained there until March 2005 when it transferred to Rainham, before moving to the new Dagenham garage in December. It stayed at Dagenham until March 2011 when it moved to First Berkshire at Slough.

Shorter 8.9m long DMS337-344 (T337-44DLR) arrived in August and were the first of twenty-five such vehicles purchased to replace the remaining midibuses in the fleet. These were followed by DMS345-348 (V345-8DLH) in October, and all twelve were allocated to Greenford. The outstanding thirteen DMS saloons (DMS349-61 V349-61DLH) were delivered in October and November. They were allocated to Orpington where they were put to use on the 336 between Bromley North and Locks Bottom.

DMS349 to 361 were superseded by twenty-three dual-door 10.2m DML class and six shorter 8.9m models DMS class, these arriving in September and October. The 10.2m saloons were numbered DML307 to DML329 (V307-20, 421, 322-9GBY) and were allocated to the First Capital operation at Hackney. They saw service on the D6 (Hackney Central-Crossharbour) and D7 (Mile End Station-Poplar).

The six shorter models were also allocated to Hackney for use on the D8 between Stratford and Crossharbour. The vehicles concerned were numbered DMS330-5, and carried registration marks V330-2, 433, 334/5GBY. A new livery was introduced on these and the DMLs, with a white and yellow band twisted along the sides, known as the 'willow leaf'.

The influx of low-floor Dart SLFs over the course of 1998 and 1999 led to the mass withdrawals of the DW class step-entrance Dart. The last DWs survived with the company until February 2002 when they departed for First Southern National.

Further 8.9m long DMS class Marshall bodied Dart SLF saloons arrived at Greenford in August 1999. DMS344 (T344ALR) is seen parked on layover just outside Greenford Broadway before heading back to Hayes on route E6. *Ian Armstrong Collection*

An order was placed in 1999 for nineteen 10.2m dual-doored Marshall Darts for use on feeder services connecting with the Croydon Tramlink. The batch was ready before the Tramway opened and were kept at Marshalls until 2000. Numbered DML362 to DML380, they were registered W362-9, 358, 371-4, 359, 376-9, 361VLN. DML363/4 arrived in February 2000 and were used as driver trainers at Orpington. DML362 followed in March and was temporarily allocated to Alperton before transferring to Orpington in April. At this time, DML379 was also loaned short-term to Alperton, both being used on the 258. Eleven of the batch were loaned to First Capital at Northumberland Park in March 2000 for use on the 212, these being DML363/5-74. In April, they moved to Dagenham, from where the T32 was initially operated. The Croydon Tramlink finally opened in May 2000, at which time the feeder services T31 (New Addington-Forestdale) and T32 (Addington-New Addington) started. By September the batch had all returned to Orpington. These vehicles wore a white and red livery to match the colour of the trams.

London Buslines DML648 (R648TLM) was withdrawn in February 2000 after suffering fire damage.

First Capital received a number of Marshall Capital bodied Dennis Dart SLFs during 2000. The first arrived in July when seven 9.3m long DM class Darts arrived. DM681 to DM687 (W681-7ULL) were allocated to Hackney Wick for use on the 308 (Wanstead-Hackney Wick). These were swiftly followed by longer DML718 to DML728 (W718/9ULL, W133VLO, W721-4ULL, W425VLO, W726/7ULL, W728VLO). Allocated to Northumberland Park, they were used on route 212 between Walthamstow and Chingford Station.

September and October were a busy couple of months for Hackney Wick garage who received a number of Marshall bodied Darts SLFs. First to arrive were DM688 to DM690 and DM697-700 (X688/9HLF, X501JLO, X697-9HLF) which initially saw service

In 1999, First London won the contract for two feeder services for the Croydon Tramlink, centred on Addington Village. It is at this location that we find DML362 (W362VLN) showing off the dedicated red and white livery applied to the vehicles for the contracts. *Ian Armstrong Collection*

on the 236 and N236 (Finsbury Park Station-Hackney Wick). They were displaced on this service in October by DML729-45 (X729HLF, X503JLO, X731-9HLF, X504JLO, X741-5HLF). The DMs then moved onto their intended service, the W11 (Walthamstow Station-Chingford, Hall Estate). They moved across to Ponders End for this route where they replaced step-entrance Alexander Dash bodied Volvo B6s. However, the allocation of DM698-700 at Ponders End was short-lived, the three transferring back to Hackney Wick in October to operate the 339 (Bow-Shadwell Station). Ponders End closed in June 2001, the W11 and W12 moving to Hackney along with the batch of Dart SLFs. DM746 to DM748 (X746-8JLO) were intended for the 339, but arriving in December 2000, they entered service on the W11 from Ponders End.

DML381 to DML402 (X381-9HLR, X78HLR, X391-9HLR, X79HLR, X401/2HLR) were the last Marshall bodied Dart SLFs to arrive with First London in 2000, doing so in October and November. Allocated to Westbourne Park, they were put to use on the 295 (Ladbrooke Grove Sainsburys-Clapham Junction). However, only three of the batch had been delivered in time for the take up of the service. The shortfall was made up of MCW Metrobuses and four Volvo B6 saloons, these working alongside DW170 and a number of DM class Dart SLFs from Westbourne Park's allocation. They were supported by four DMLs from Alperton. DML384 was the last to arrive in December. The 295 was double-decked in 2002, at which time the DMLs were transferred to Greenford.

2001 started with the delivery of twenty-two DMLs to First Capital, these arriving in January. The batch was numbered DML751 to DML772 and carried registration marks X751JLO, X752-4, 506, 756-9, 507, 761-4, 508, 766-9, 509, 771/2HLR. Hackney Wick took delivery of the batch and put them to use on the 257 (Stratford-Walthamstow) and 296 (Ilford High Road-Romford Station). In November, the 257 was converted to double-deck operation. DML751 to DML764 were then transferred to Dagenham where

As has been seen in the last few photographs, the allocation of Darts at the former Hackney and later Lea Interchange garages of First London were rather fluid. DM41700 (DM700-X502JLO) was new to First London for routes 236 and 399. However, it is seen operating route 309 whilst negotiating Canning Town bus station. *Liam Farrer-Beddall*

they were used on the 165 between Romford Market and Rainham. The Dagenham operation was moved to Rainham in March 2002. DML756 and 758 were transferred to Centrewest.

These were followed by sixteen shorter DM class Dart SLFs in February. Northumberland Park was the recipient of this batch which were used on the 299 (Muswell Hill Broadway-Cockfosters), W6 (Southgate Station-Edmonton Green) and W10 (Enfield Town-Crews Hill Station). The vehicles in question were numbered DM773 to DM788 (X773/4, 511, 776, 512, 778/9, 513, 781-5, 514, 787/8HLR).

London Buslines lost the 490 in April 2001 when eight DMLs transferred from Southall to Uxbridge where they were used on the U3. A second blow to the Southall Dart operation came in June when the 105 was converted to double-deck operation. After this time, the DMLs transferred to Greenford, with DMs being reallocated to Uxbridge. During the same month, eleven DMLs transferred from London Buslines after that operation was wound down. This led to DM129-137 being transferred to Uxbridge for use on the 331.

Further Dart SLF movements took place in the autumn of 2001. DMS349, 352/3 and 356 transferred to First Capital at Northumberland Park, where they were mostly used on the 318. At the same time, DMS355/8/60/1 were transferred to Orpington.

The closing months of 2001 saw the arrival of twenty-nine DML class Dart SLFs with Centrewest. The first eight arrived in October and were allocated to Uxbridge. They were used on the 331 between Uxbridge Station and Ruislip Station. Rolling stock numbers DML403 to DML410 were allocated to the batch which carried cherished Routemaster registrations 133CLT, 292CLT, 503CLT, WLT659, 676DYE, 809-11DYE. They displaced a batch of Plaxton Pointer bodied Dennis Darts on the route.

Similar vehicles were displaced at Orpington by the arrival of DML411 to DML414 (LK51JYJ/L/N/O), these being used on the R9. 411 to 413 were still allocated to Orpington at the time of the sale to Metrobus in December 2007, DML414 having transferred to Willesden Junction.

Thirty-five Marshall Capital bodied Dennis Dart SLFs were allocated to Alperton during October and November 2001. First were the final seventeen DMLs which were allocated to routes 224 (Willesden Junction-Wembley) and 226 (Golders Green Station-Park Royal). These displaced the DW class from these services. The batch transferred to the newly opened Willesden Junction garage in March 2004. These vehicles were numbered DML415 to DML431 (LN51DWY/Z, DXA-H/J-M/O/P/U).

Eighteen shorter DM class Dart SLFs, DM432-449, completed the deliveries in November. These were split between routes 223, PR1 and PR2 respectively. Registration marks LN51DWV/W/X, DVW-Z, DVO/P/R/T/V, DUA/H/J/U/V/Y were carried by these vehicles. They also transferred to Willesden Junction with the services in March 2004.

The final deliveries were received in December, these being six shorter DMS class Dart SLFs which were allocated to Dagenham. DMS790 to DMS795 (LN51GJV/X/Y/Z, GOP/U) were used on the W19 between Walthamstow and Ilford High Road. However, they were also found on the 296 and 396 when required. They transferred to the temporary Rainham garage in March 2002 before returning to the new Dagenham garage in December 2005.

Twenty-four 8.9m long DMS class Dart SLFs arrived between February and March 2002. These were numbered DMS450 to DMS473 (LN51DVA-C/F, RZZ, SBO/U/V, LT02ZDM-P/R/S/U/V/W/X, ZDA/C/D/E/F/G). Seven of the batch were used on newly won service 273 (Lewisham to Petts Wood Station) from Stagecoach London. This introduced First London into new operating territory in the Chislehurst and Grove Park areas. At the same time Orpington area local services R1 and R11 also gained new rolling stock.

The final eighteen Marshall Capital bodied Dart SLF saloons were taken into stock during 2002. However, during 2002 Marshall entered administration which caused problems for First London. The Company had ordered a batch for the 364 and 499.

Northumberland Park took delivery of sixteen short DM class Dart SLF saloons in February 2001. They were shared between routes 299, W6 and W10. DM41778 (X778HLR) is seen on layover at Edmonton Green Bus Station whilst operating the W6. *Liam Farrer-Beddall*

DML412 (LK51JYL) is seen having just left Orpington town centre, heading towards nearby Orpington Station on route R9. *Collin Lloyd/Jeff Lloyd Collection*

DMS487 to DMS489 (LT02ZDY/Z, ZFA) arrived at Greenford in June, with four more arriving in July at Rainham. These took up rolling stock numbers DMS474, 476-8 (LT02NUK/O/P/U). DMS490/1 (LT02ZFB/C) also arrived in July and were also allocated to Greenford. To cover the shortfall, a number of DMs and DMLs were transferred from other First London garages. Seven more arrived at Greenford in August. These were numbered DMS475/9-84 (LT02NUM, NUV, NVE/F/G/H/J). The final pair also arrived in August, being allocated to Northumberland Park. DMS485 and DMS486 (LT02NUW/X) were used on the 379, entering service on this route in September.

The Marshall bodied Dart SLFs began to leave London in 2002, being cascaded to First's provincial operations. New contracts began to specify new buses and, after Marshalls ceased to be available, First London began to take Caetano Nimbus Darts. After them came new Enviro 200s.

The collapse of Marshall meant that First London had to find a new body supplier for the Dart SLF. The Company chose the 10.5m Caetano Nimbus body. Deliveries of the type commenced in the spring of 2003, with a second batch arriving in the autumn. The first twenty-nine arrived between March and August and were allocated to Rainham. The class code DHL was used. They carried on from the Marshall Darts, being numbered DHL492 to DHL525 (LK03LMJ, LLX/Z, LME/F, LNU, NLN, LNV/W/X, NLD/E/F/G/J/L/M/T, NFY/Z, NGE/F/G, UEX-Z, UFA-C). They were ordered for the 364 (Ilford High Road-Dagenham East) and 499 (Romford High Road-Becontree Heath-Romford). However, they were also used on the 165, 296 and W19. In December 2005, Rainham garage closed, the fleet moving to Dagenham.

The second batch was allocated to Uxbridge, the first of which arrived in September 2003, delivery being completed by November. They were used on the U2 (Uxbridge Station-Hillingdon Hospital) and U3 (Uxbridge Station-Hayes), and shortly after

DHL512 (LK03NGE) shows off the smart Caetano Nimbus body style. It is photographed behind Romford Station whilst operating the 296 between Romford and Ilford. *David Beddall*

arrival they saw service on the A10 (Uxbridge Station-Heathrow Airport Central), along with the U1, U10 and 331. They were mixed in with the Marshall Capital bodied Dart SLFs.

First UK bus operations were renumbered into a five-digit numbering system in 2003. Unlike Stagecoach, each operating company within First were renumbered at different times during the year. In October, the London operations were renumbered. Under this, L1 to L6 were renumbered DMP42401-6, whilst the Marshall Capital and Caetano Nimbus bodied Dart SLFs were numbered 41###, retaining their original class codes. Five of the Caetano Nimbus bodied Darts were renumbered DMC42515-9 after First numbered a new batch of Dart SLFs 41515-9. These vehicles had originally been numbered this, but rather than renumber the other vehicles, the London Darts were renumbered.

First London lost the contract for the T31 to Arriva London South in May 2007 but retained the T32. This latter route required three vehicles which were retained at Orpington, these being DML41373/4/5/80. The others (DML41362-41380) were refurbished and reallocated to Greenford and Alperton.

A number of the Dagenham batch transferred across to Uxbridge after the introduction of new Enviro 200 saloons. 41503-6 and 41513 moved across in November 2007, followed by 41511 in May 2008, and 41507-10 in June. 41492/4-500/2 were briefly transferred to Greenford in March 2009 for use on the 195 after this route was taken on by the Company at short notice. They stayed there for a month before moving across to Lea Interchange, replacing older Marshall bodied Dart SLFs.

First London briefly operated a Marshall Capital bodied Dennis Dart SLF registered S979JLM. This vehicle carried rolling stock number DMS43800 and was acquired in mid-September 2004 from First Essex. It returned to First Essex in October. It wore the provincial corporate First livery for the duration of its stay at Dagenham. S979JLM was new as a demonstrator with Marshalls of Cambridge.

Hackney Wick garage closed in December 2007 to make way for the construction of the Olympic Village for the London 2012 Olympic Games. The fleet based at this garage transferred to Lea Interchange.

The same month saw the operations at Orpington sold to Metrobus, with the transfer of twenty-eight Dart SLFs. The vehicles transferred were DMS41450-67 which became 124-131, 138-147 and 132-137. Seven longer DMLs (41411-3, 41375/80/73/4) were also transferred, these becoming 380-6. All were reallocated to Metrobus' Green Street Green garage.

First operated two bus routes replacing trains during the rebuild of the East London line for the Overground. One of the routes, ELW, was at first operated by double-decks, but poor patronage resulted in the substitution by seven DMS class Darts. Route branding for the service was applied to the batch of seven (DMS41258/60/1, 41350/1/2/4). The branding was located on a yellow cantrail, with orange panels being placed next to the destination display. The service commenced operation in August 2008.

First Group sold off most of its London operations in June 2013, with Metroline, Go-Ahead London and new operator Tower Transit benefitting from this. The operations and vehicles taken over by these three companies can be found under the relevant headings in this book.

STAGECOACH LONDON

East London and Selkent were both acquired by Stagecoach Holdings PLC on 6 September 1994. They were operated as separate companies but for the purpose of this book, they are grouped together. A large number of Dennis Darts, bodied by Carlyle, Wright and Plaxton, were acquired from London Buses limited.

The Carlyle Dartlines acquired came from the Selkent operation, and were numbered DT28, 30-40 and 55, all of which were being used in the Orpington area. They wore an all-over red livery relieved by white Stagecoach fleet names. Two small batches of Wrightbus Handybus bodied Darts were acquired. East London were operating DW133 to DW159 and DWL15-26, all being allocated to Barking garage. DW59-65 and 71 were operating with Selkent south of the river. The final Darts to be acquired from London Buses Limited were a sizable batch of Pointer Darts. DRL109 to DRL146 were all operated by East London and were shared between Barking, Stratford and Upton Park.

1994 proved to be relatively quiet in terms of the Dennis Dart fleet with both companies. DW159 received an all-blue livery in October, for use on a contract service to the Tesco store at Barking. It retained this livery until November 1997 when it was replaced by DRL121 (K121SRH) on the contract.

In the opening months of 1995, Stagecoach East London won one of the contracts for the East London Line rail replacement service whilst the line was upgraded. For this, several SR class midibuses were put to use on this contract. To cover the loss of these midibuses at Stratford, DW133-5/7/9, 141/5-7, 151/2/4/7/8 were transferred from Barking, this taking place during March.

A couple of months later, in July, Barking lost ten Plaxton Pointer bodied Dennis Darts. At this time, DRL109-12/4/8 and 123/36-8 were transferred to North Street, Romford where they were used on the 247 and 499. They had been replaced at Barking by longer LA class Alexander PS bodied Dennis Lance saloons.

By 1995, the Alexander Dash had become a popular body style for the Stagecoach Group and featured in many of its fleets across the country on both the Dennis Dart and Volvo B6 chassis. A number of Alexander Dash bodied Dennis Darts were taken into stock by Stagecoach London. The first twenty-seven arrived with East London between August and October. The first eleven, DAL1 to DAL11 (N301-11AMC), were allocated to North Street, Romford where they were used on the 247 between Barkingside Station, Hainault, Collier Row and Romford Station. The other sixteen were allocated to Barking and were numbered DAL12 to DAL27 (N312-27AMC).

DW159 (NDZ3159) received an all-over blue livery in 1994 for use on a contract service to the Tesco store in Barking. It is seen wearing this livery when photographed. *Collin Lloyd/Jeff Lloyd Collection*

They were used on the 238 (Stratford-East Ham-Barking-Barking Garage). DAL1-9 were transferred from Romford to Leyton in June 1996, where they were used on the 230 (Wood Green-Upper Walthamstow).

DT32, 34 and 37 were transferred from Orpington to Bromley in October 1995. They were used by the latter garage on the seasonal Bromley Park & Ride service. Stagecoach Selkent lost its contracts in the Orpington area in November and December 1995 to Centrewest. This led to the cascade of the DT class Darts to neighbouring Selkent garages. DT35 joined the three mentioned at Bromley, whilst Catford gained DT39 in November, followed by DT28, 30/1/3/6/8 and 40 in December, this completing the rundown of the Roundabout operation in Orpington. The transfer of these Darts led to the withdrawal of older Mercedes-Benz minibuses at Catford. DT30 was the last Dennis Dart to operate on the Orpington area services with Stagecoach.

Thirty-nine Alexander Dash bodied Dennis Darts were ordered by Stagecoach and allocated south of the river to the Selkent operation. These featured a modified front-end grille as can be seen in the photograph below. Unlike their counterparts operating with Stagecoach East London, the Selkent Dash bodied Darts did not carry the DAL classification code, instead they were numbered using a three-digit number. 601 to 604 (N601-4KGF) were first to arrive, putting in an appearance during December 1995. Intended for Plumstead, they were delivered to Bromley for use on the Christmas Park & Ride service. These were followed in January 1996 by 605 to 614 (N605-14KGF). These entered service from Plumstead on route 177 (Peckham-New Cross-Greenwich-Woolwich-Plumstead-Abbey Wood Station). 615 to 639 were not delivered until September and November 1996. 616 to 625 (P616-25PGP) were allocated to Catford where they were used on the 160 (Catford-Eltham-New Eltham-Chislehurst-Sidcup Station). 615 and 626 to 639 (P615/26-39PGP) joined the first fourteen Darts at Plumstead where they were used on the 202 (Crystal Palace-Sydenham-Catford-Lee Green-Blackheath).

The first new Dennis Darts to enter the Stagecoach London fleet were allocated to North Street, Romford for the 247. DAL5 (N305AMC) is seen at Romford Station whilst off route, operating the 499. They later transferred to Leyton for use on the 230. *Ian Armstrong Collection*

Another thirty-nine Alexander Dash bodied Dennis Darts were purchased for the Selkent operation. 615 to 639 were allocated to Catford featuring a revised front grille. They were ordered for use on the 160 and 202. 618 (P618PGP) is seen parked at Sidcup Station. *Ian Armstrong Collection*

The first low-floor Alexander ALX200 bodied Dennis Dart SLFs arrived with Stagecoach East London in September 1996. They were allocated to Leyton for use on the 230, with added route branding for this service. SLD7 (P27HMF) is seen on layover in Bisterne Avenue, Walthamstow showing this branding. The low-floor credentials of the bus are also noted at the rear of SLD7. *Ian Armstrong Collection*

Alexander replaced the Dash with the stylish ALX200 model. Stagecoach London was the first operator of this new type in London. Stagecoach used the SLD class code for both the Alexander ALX200 and Plaxton Pointer models, the exception being made for thirteen ALX200s taken into stock for the London City Airport contract. SLD1-9 (P21-9HMF) were the first of the type to be delivered to the Company, arriving in September and October 1996. Measuring 10.2m in length, these nine single-doored vehicles were allocated to Stagecoach East London's Leyton garage. They were put to use on the 230 carrying appropriate branding, replacing step-entrance Alexander Dash bodied Darts on this service.

In 1997, Stagecoach London were successful in gaining the contract for a service between Liverpool Street Station and London City Airport. They took over the service a month earlier than planned, taking it on in March 1997. For this contract, Stagecoach ordered a batch of Alexander ALX200 bodied Dennis Dart SLFs. However, these were late arriving. To cover whilst the Company awaited the delivery of these new vehicles, DRL class Darts filled in. Whilst these Darts operated in red, two of them, DRL125/6, were repainted in all-over blue for use on the service, both being given route branding.

The seven ALX200s ordered arrived in March 1997. As mentioned above, this batch did not receive the standard SLD class code, instead being classified LCY. The batch took up stock numbers LCY1 to LCY7 and were registered P801-7NJN. They were allocated to Stratford and wore a blue livery similar to that applied to the DRLs, complete with white lettering.

Transit Holdings Ltd, who had operations in Devon, Oxford, Portsmouth and London, was acquired by Stagecoach on 22 July 1997. The London operations traded

as Docklands Minibus who had by this time purchased eighteen Plaxton Pointer bodied Dennis Darts, full details of which feature later in this book. However, just to record them here, N410-27MBW were taken into stock by Stagecoach East London and numbered PD410-27.

Under the control of London Buses Limited, the Selkent division never operated the Plaxton Pointer bodied Dennis Dart. Five members of this type were transferred from East London to Catford garage in August 1997. The vehicles concerned were DRL110/7/8 and 123/7.

Further new rolling stock arrived over the course of July and August 1997. At this time SLD10-9 (P610/1SEV, R712XAR, P613SEV, R114-9VPU) were allocated to Barking, from where they were used on the 364 between Ilford High Road and Dagenham East.

August also saw the arrival of the first low-floor buses for Selkent, these being numbered SLD20 to SLD23 (R120-3VPU). These were followed by SLD24 to SLD29 (R124-9VPU) in September. They were allocated to Bromley where they replaced Optare MetroRiders on route 314 between Eltham and New Addington.

DT34, 36 and 37 were transferred in August from Selkent to the newly acquired Docklands Minibus operation. In September, members of the DT class were withdrawn from London service and cascaded to other Stagecoach operations around the country, with the majority transferring to Stagecoach Devon and Stagecoach Red & White. The type had disappeared from Stagecoach London by June 1998. Just prior to this, DRL128 to DRL132 were transferred to Catford to allow this to happen.

The last new batch of step-entrance Dennis Darts arrived in September 1997. PD1 to PD18 (R701-18YWC) were taken into stock to replace the former Dennis Darts that had been acquired from Docklands Minibus on route 106 and were allocated to Stratford. The former Docklands Minibus Darts were reallocated around Stagecoach London for further use.

Service enhancements on the London City Airport contract resulted in two additional ALX200 bodied Dart SLFs being ordered by Stagecoach. These arrived in September 1997 at which time they took fleet numbers LCY8 and LCY9 (R208/9XNO). They were also painted into a blue livery for the contract, joining the original seven at Stratford.

Stagecoach East London lost the contract for route S2 (Clapton, Nightingale Road-Stratford Bus Station) in February 1998, the service passing to Capital Citybus. Following the loss, DW133 to DW137 moved south of the river from Stratford to Plumstead where they were used on the 380.

Withdrawals of the Alexander Dash bodied Dennis Darts began in January 1998 when these single-doored saloons were exchanged with Stagecoach Oxford for dual-doored Plaxton Pointer bodied Darts. In total, forty-one Alexander Dash bodied Darts were exchanged. PD712/6, 718-21, carrying registration marks L712JUD etc arrived in January. These were soon followed by PD709-11, 713-5/7 and 722 (L709JUD etc) in February. With the exception of PD722, which entered service at Plumstead, these vehicles were originally allocated to Barking.

Further Pointer Darts arrived from Stagecoach Oxford in the following months. March 1998 saw the arrival of PD63-5/7-9, 71/3 (M63VJO etc), with PD81-3/5-7/9, 91/2 (M81MBW etc) arriving during the same month. Barking took delivery of PD63 and PD64, whilst the others entered service from Plumstead. However, in April PDs 65, 78 and 722 were transferred from Plumstead to Barking. PD86 and 91 also made the journey north during April, being allocated to Stratford. PD102 (M102WBW) was next to put in an appearance, arriving at Plumstead during May. The transfer of PDs between East London and Selkent continued during September when PD69 moved to Barking, although this was short lived, returning to Plumstead the following month.

Replacements for PD401-427 arrived in September 1997 when a similar number of step-entrance Plaxton Pointer bodied Dennis Dart saloons were delivered to Stagecoach East London. They were allocated to Stratford for use on the 106. PD10 (R710YWC) is seen parked at Finsbury Park Station, showing the split-step layout of the entrance. *Ian Armstrong Collection*

Former Thames Transit, Oxford M92WBW is captured by the camera in Woolwich town centre. Numbered PD92, it is seen heading towards Abbey Wood Station on route 177, being allocated to nearby Plumstead garage. *Collin Lloyd/Jeff Lloyd Collection*

Alongside these second-hand Darts, Stagecoach London also took delivery of twelve ALX200 bodied Dart SLFs at Stratford between March and April. The vehicles concerned were numbered SLD30 to SLD41 (R930-41FOO). These were used on the 276 (East Beckton-Stoke Newington Common). A second contract to London City Airport, this time from Canning Town, commenced in October 1999. For this, SLD30 to SLD32 were used on this new service. They received a green livery with route branding to help distinguish between this new service and the existing one to Liverpool Street.

Seventeen shorter 9.4m ALX200 bodied Dart SLFs were delivered to Stagecoach in April and May 1998. The first eight, SLD42-9 (R942-9FOO), arrived at Catford in April. They were used on the P4 between Lewisham Station and Brixton. At the same time SLD50 (R950FOO) was delivered to Stratford, followed by SLD51 to SLD58 (R451-8FVX) in May. These were used on the 100 between Liverpool Street and Shadwell Station.

The final PDs from Stagecoach Oxford arrived between September and December 1998. PD103 (M103WBW) arrived at Plumstead during September. It was joined there in November by PD93 to PD95 (M93-5WBW). The final example arrived during December and took up stock number PD96 (M96WBW).

The London City Airport contract fleet was strengthened in October 1998 when another two ALX200 bodied Dart SLFs arrived. Numbered LCY10 and LCY11 (S410/1TNO) they were allocated to Stratford.

Thirty new ALX200s were delivered to Stagecoach London between November 1998 and January 1999. They were split between Bromley and Plumstead. Fourteen of these, SLD59 to SLD72 (S459-72BWC), were allocated to Bromley where they were used on the 269 (Bexleyheath Shopping Centre-Bromley North). Plumstead took delivery of SLD73 to SLD88 (S473-88BWC), these entering service on the 99 (Woolwich-Erith), won from London Central. Those delivered in January 1999 were used on the 178 (Woolwich-Kidbrooke) and 291 (Woolwich-Woodlands Estate).

March 1997 saw Stagecoach win the contract for a service linking London City Airport and Liverpool Street Station. For this seven Alexander ALX200s were ordered, taking the class code LCY. The service grew over the following years, resulting in eleven vehicles being operated by 1998. LCY11 (S411TNO) represents the type, seen at London City Airport in the blue livery. *Ian Armstrong Collection*

The D3 (Bethnal Green-Crossharbour) was due to receive a new batch of ALX200 bodied Dart SLFs, SLD89-95 (S489-95BWC), but this did not come to fruition. Instead, SLD89 was allocated to Bromley, whilst SLD90 to SLD94 were allocated to North Street, Romford where they were used on the 247 (Romford-Barkingside). SLD89 was soon swapped for SLD94. This batch was built to single-door layout. SLD89-92 were delivered in January 1999, whilst SLD93-5 arrived in February.

SLD96 to SLD106 (S496-9BWC, S210WHK, S101-6WHK) were allocated to Stratford in February, where they were mostly used on the 309 (Canning Town-Bethnal Green), also seeing service on the 100. These were also the last Alexander ALX200 bodied Dart SLFs to be purchased by Stagecoach London until 2001.

Between 1999 and 2001, Stagecoach London took delivery of 130 Plaxton Pointer bodied Dennis Dart SLFs. The first of the type arrived with the Company during the autumn of 1999 when four were delivered to North Street, Romford. Upon arrival, SLD107-110 (V107-10MVX) completed the allocation of Dennis Dart SLFs on route 247.

The first dual-doored Pointer Dart SLFs arrived in November, being allocated to Stagecoach East London. Rolling stock numbers SLD111 to SLD140 (V173, 112-20, 174, 122-140MVX) were given to this batch of thirty vehicles. SLD111-22 were allocated to Stratford, whilst Barking took delivery of the rest. Those at Stratford were used on the 276 (Newnham Hospital-Stoke Newington Common), the Barking contingent being used on the 300 between Canning Town and East Ham, and the 325 (Prince Regent Station-Beckton).

An additional thirty-two Pointer Darts were delivered to East London between November 1999 and January 2000. They carried on from the previous batch as SLD141 to SLD172 (V141-172MVX). Stratford took delivery of SLD141-155 and SLD164-172,

February 1999 saw the arrival of eleven ALX200 bodied Dart SLFs at Stratford for use on the 309. The last of the batch, SLD106 (S106WHK), is seen heading towards Bethnal Green. *Ian Armstrong Collection*

whilst Upton Park took SLD156 to SLD163. Those at the latter garage were primarily used on route 376 between Beckton and East Ham. Those at Stratford covered the extension of route 100 from Liverpool Street to Elephant & Castle, as well as restocking the 309.

Fifty-one Pointer Darts were delivered between May and July 2000. The first twenty-three, SLD173 to SLD195 (W173-95DNO), were added to Upton Park's allocation. They were ordered for routes 104 and 238, replacing step-entrance Scania double-decks, but could be found operating on any of the single-deck routes from this garage.

The remainder of this sizable batch of Pointer Darts were allocated south of the river, to the Selkent division. The batch was numbered SLD196 to SLD223 and were registered W196-9, 233, 201-21, 236, 223DNO. Bromley took delivery of SLD196 to SLD203, and SLD212 to SLD219. Catford was the recipient of SLD204 to SLD211 and SLD220-223. Those at Catford were used on the 225 for a short while, until the route was lost to London Central in the spring of 2001. Bromley lost its allocation of this batch of Dart SLFs in February 2001. SLD196-203 moved across to Catford at this time where they were used on the 181, 284 and P4. At the same time SLD212 to SLD219 transferred to Plumstead.

A batch of thirteen longer 11.3m Pointer Darts were allocated to Bromley in December 2000. SLD224-236 (X224, 237, 226-9, 238, 231-6NNO) were put to use on the 227 (Crystal Palace-Bromley North). They replaced step-entrance Plaxton Verde bodied Dennis Lance saloons that had been in use on the service since 1994. The batch stayed true to the 227, operating the service until 2012 when they were replaced by Mercedes-Benz Citaros.

Transport for London had, by 2001, a preference for dual-doored buses where possible. An impressive ninety-one Alexander ALX200s were purchased by Stagecoach London during 2001. Seventeen measured 8.9m, the other seventy-four measuring

Further Pointer Darts were received between November 1999 and January 2000 at Stratford, mostly for the 100 and 309. 34147 (SLD147-V147MVX) was one of this batch. It is seen passing St Paul's Cathedral bound for Shadwell Station on route 100. By this time it had received the new Stagecoach livery introduced to the fleet in 2001. *Gary Seamarks*

2000 saw a number of Pointer Darts allocated to the Selkent operations. SLD220 (W235DNO) is one of those allocated to Bromley. It is seen parked at Eltham Station whilst working the 162. *Ian Armstrong Collection*

December 2000 saw thirteen Pointer Darts allocated to Bromley for use on the 227. 34224 (X224WNO) was one of this batch, which stayed on the service until replaced by new rolling stock in 2012. 34224 is photographed in Bromley approaching journey's end at Bromley North. *Liam Farrer-Beddall*

10.2m. They were used to replace the early batches of single-doored Dart SLFs, along with the remaining step-entrance DAL class Darts.

The shorter 8.8m examples arrived in May 2001 and took stock numbers SLD237 to SLD253. Registered Y237-9, 347, 241-4, 348, 245-9, 349, 251-3FJN, they were allocated to Catford from where they operated the 124 (Catford-Eltham) and 273 (Lewisham-Petts Wood). Stagecoach UK Bus got a new livery in January 2001. The red livery worn by Stagecoach London featured a dark-blue skirt with an orange and lighter blue swoop at the rear of the vehicle. A new rolling ball logo was also introduced.

These were followed by thirty-six more numbered SLD254-289 (Y254, 351, 256-9, 352, 261-5, 366, 267-9, 353, 271-4, 354, 276/7FJN, LX51FPE, Y279, 356, 281-7FJN, Y671USG and Y289FJN). These were allocated to Barking and were delivered between July and September 2001. SLD288 (Y671USG) was loaned to Stagecoach Fife between September 2001 and March 2002 and was registered in Scotland. The next thirteen to arrive were SLD290-302 (LX51FFW, Y291-9FJN, LX51FPJ, Y301/2FJN). These also arrived over August and September, with the exception of SLD300 which put in an appearance in November. Leyton took delivery of this batch which was used on route 230.

Catford was allocated SLD303-312 (LX51FGA/F/E/D/G/M/K/V/J/N) when they arrived in September. Route 284 was the intended service for this batch, although they could also be found operating routes P4 and 181. The final batch arrived in September and October 2001; these being numbered SLD313 to SLD327 (LX51FGO/P/U/Z, FHG/B/A/C/D/E/F/K/L/H/J). Plumstead took delivery of this batch which was put to use on the 202. These were amongst the last ALX200s to be delivered to Stagecoach London.

Slotted in amongst these were a batch of 10.8m long ALX200s, these arriving in May and June 2001. SLD328 to SLD346 (Y371, 329, 372, 331/2, 373, 334-9, 374FJN, LX51FFO, Y342-6FJN) were all allocated to Barking for use on the 62 (Barking-Marks Gate) and 145 (Dagenham-Leytonstone).

September and October 2001 saw the arrival of a small batch of Alexander ALX200 bodied Dennis Dart SLFs at Catford. They were used mostly on the 284, which is the route we find SLD307 (LX51FGG) on. It is captured by the camera at Lewisham Station. *Ian Armstrong Collection*

To help distinguish between the different lengths of Dart SLFs in the fleet, Stagecoach London reclassified the SLDs into four different class codes in June 2002. The DSS class code was used for the shortest models, measuring 8.8m. Next was the DS class which was applied to the Dart SLFs that measured 9.3m or 9.4m in length. The next length, 10.1m, were classified as DM. The longest Dart SLFs were classified DL, these measuring either 10.8m or 11.3m in length. To summarise, the new fleet numbers applied to the Dart SLF fleet were DM30-41, DS42-58, DM59-78, DS79-88, DM89-95, DS96-106, DM107-138, DS139-172, DM173-203, DS204-223, DL224-236, DSS237-253, DM254-327 and DL328-346. By this time, SLD1 to SLD29 had been cascaded within the Stagecoach Group.

Deliveries of Dart SLFs resumed in November 2002 after a gap of a year and a half. Seventeen 10.1m long Pointer Darts arrived and were split between Barking and Bromley. DM347 to DM353 (LV52HJY/Z, HKA-E) were the batch allocated to Barking, being put to use on the 396. Bromley took delivery of DM354 to DM365. They continued the registration series on from the Barking batch as LV52HKF-H/J-P/T/U. They were used on the 314. By this time, the Dennis Dart SLF had been rebranded as the Transbus Dart.

Eleven shorter 8.8m long Pointer MPDs arrived at Plumstead in January 2003. DSS366 to DSS376 (LV52HGC-G/J-O) were the vehicles concerned and were used on the 380 between Belmarsh Prison and Lewisham. These were the last Darts to be numbered in this series.

Stagecoach renumbered its UK bus and coach fleet into a single five-digit numbering system in the same month. Losing their class prefixes, LCY1-11 were given new numbers, 33351-61; whilst the main fleet of Darts were numbered 34###. However, Stagecoach applied the letters L, M, S and X to help distinguish between the different lengths.

The first Transbus Pointer Darts to be delivered with the new fleet numbers arrived in March. They were numbered 34377 to 34386 (LX03BZJ-N/P/R-U). Allocated to Plumstead, they were used on the 386 between Greenwich, Blackheath and Woolwich. These vehicles measured 9.3m in length.

These were soon followed by eleven 10.1m long Transbus Darts. Arriving in April, they took up stock numbers 34387 to 34397. Registered LX03BZV/W/Y, CAA/E/U/V, CBF/U/V/Y, they were initially allocated to Catford for use on the P4, replacing the single-doored Dart SLFs, but could be found on other services from their home garage.

By the time the final batch of ten Transbus Pointer Darts arrived in December 2003, Stagecoach had invested heavily in new Transbus Pointer Darts for its provincial operations. These vehicles slotted in between 34397 and the new London batch, 34551 to 34560 (LX53LGF/G/J/K/L/N/O/U/V/W). They were initially allocated to Plumstead for use on the 178. In March 2006, the 178 and the batch of vehicles moved across to Catford.

The original batch of Dennis Dart SLFs used on the London City Airport contracts were replaced by newer Plaxton Pointer bodied Dart SLFs in the summer of 2003. 34193 and 34195 were first to be repainted blue in May, followed by 34183/4/7/8/9/91/2/4 in June, also being repainted in the blue livery. 34182 was the final Dart to receive the blue livery, this being done in September. 34194 and 34197 were repainted in the green version of the livery in June, joined by 34196 in September. All were down seated from B31D to B29D, with additional luggage space being fitted.

The withdrawal of the ALX200s from the London City Airport contracts saw 33351 to 33356 converted to driver training vehicles, remaining in use until 2005. At this time,

Eleven 10.1m Dart SLFs with Transbus Pointer bodies arrived in March 2003. They were again allocated to Plumstead and used on the 386. 34380 (LX03BZM) is seen passing through Woolwich bound for Blackheath Village. *Liam Farrer-Beddall*

The final batch of Transbus Pointer Darts was taken into stock in December 2003 for use on the 178. 34553 (LX53LGJ) is seen in Woolwich town centre, heading towards Lewisham. They were received in the new corporate livery but lost it in favour of 100 per cent red livery. *Liam Farrer-Beddall*

A trio of Pointer Darts also received the green London City Airport livery. 34196 (W196DNO) was one of these vehicles. It is seen attending the 2004 North Weald bus rally. *David Beddall*

The spring of 2015 saw four Transbus Darts added to the Stagecoach London training fleet. 34358 (LV52HKK) is seen parked at West Ham garage. Stagecoach painted this fleet into the 2001 Stagecoach livery to distinguish these vehicles from the service buses. *Aethan Blake*

they transferred to Stagecoach Warwickshire. 33357 to 33361 passed to Stagecoach South in 2003.

Between November 2005 and June 2006, a number of loans took place. Four Pointer Darts were loaned from Transdev London for the 2005 Bromley Park & Ride service. Bromley took delivery of DPS664 to DPS667 (LG03FGN/O/P/U) and SDP539 (V539JBH) in November, these remaining in use until the end of December.

Bromley based 34212-4/7/8, 220-3 were placed on loan to Arriva Kent Thameside at Dartford during March 2006 for use on the 162. They returned to Stagecoach in April 2006. At the same time, 34119 to 34123 were loaned to Travel London for use on the 152. These also returned to Stagecoach in June, at which time they were withdrawn.

Australian banking group Macquaire Bank purchased the operations of Stagecoach London in June 2006. This introduced a new company to London, the East London Bus Group. This new company continued to use the East London and Selkent fleet names. The early Alexander ALX200 bodied Dart SLFs had been sold to other Stagecoach operators by 2006. 34117, 34147-50/2/6-9, 34161-181, 34190/6, 34198-211, 34222-397, 34551-560 were transferred to this new operator. Details of the fleet under the ownership of East London can be found under that heading later in this book.

However, the East London Bus Group was a short-lived operation, with Stagecoach acquiring it in October 2010. By this time, the fleet had seen some investment, but a number of older Dart SLFs were still operating in service. However, Stagecoach soon set out to modernise the fleet, with a large number of Enviro 200 saloons arriving during 2011.

Darts on routes 124 and 227 were replaced by newer rolling stock in 2012.

Four Transbus Darts, 34353 (LV52HKE), 34355 (LV52HKG), 34357/8 (LV52HKJ/K), were converted to driver training vehicles in March 2015. These became the last Darts to leave Stagecoach London in the summer of 2019. The driver training fleet were painted into the 2001 style Stagecoach London livery.

GO-AHEAD LONDON

The current (2021) Go-Ahead London operation is made up of five operating companies, London Central, London General, Blue Triangle, Docklands Buses and Metrobus. London Central was the first company to be acquired by the Go-Ahead Group on 22 September 1994. London General was originally purchased by its management on 2 November 1994. It was not until 23 May 1996 that the Company was purchased by Go-Ahead. However, London General is covered under this title from November 1994. The remaining operating companies joined the Go-Ahead London Group much later, and acquisition dates will be included later in this section.

Unlike the other former London Buses Limited subsidiaries, London Central took a mere twenty-seven Dennis Darts into stock at the time of privatisation. Sixteen of these carried Plaxton Pointer bodies. DRL1 to DRL16 were initially allocated to Peckham, but in April 1995 they transferred across to Bexleyheath where they displaced SR class midibuses, which moved in the opposite direction. The DRLs remained in service until the summer of 2000 when they were withdrawn. The other eleven Darts carried the East Lancs EL2000 body style. DEL1-11 (L901-11JRN) were allocated to Camberwell where they were used on the 484 and P5. London Central was the only red bus operator to take delivery of this type, these remaining in service until May 2001 when they were sold to a dealer.

In comparison, London General were operating a large fleet of Dennis Darts in south-west London at the time of privatisation. Both the DR and DRL class Pointer Darts featured in the fleet. Those acquired were numbered DR32-9, 41/3-52 and 149-53, these being shared between Putney, Battersea Bridge midibus base and Merton. DRL54 to DRL95 were the longer Pointer Darts transferred to London General ownership, these being shared between Battersea Bridge and Stockwell. In addition, the Company was operating a number of Wrightbus Handybus bodied Darts. DW44-8, 66-70, 127-32 and 160/1 were operating under the *Streetline* brand from Merton and Sutton at this time.

Little investment in terms of single-deck rolling stock was made by London Central and London General in the early years. A small batch of sixteen 9.25m long Plaxton Pointer bodied Darts was purchased by London General in 1995. DPL1 to DPL16 (M201-16EGF) were allocated to Merton in June for use on routes 200 and 201.

The purchase of London General by the Go-Ahead Group in May 1996 led to numerous transfers of vehicles between London General and London Central. A number of Handybus bodied Darts were transferred in June 1998. DW45-8, 52, 66, 70, 127/8, 131 and 160/1 passed to London Central who allocated them to Peckham.

Despite numerous changes to the Plaxton Pointer model over the years, the type proved popular with Go-Ahead London. Between London Central and London

London General took delivery of the first new Dennis Darts, these arriving in June 1995 at Merton, carrying Plaxton Pointer bodywork. They were ordered against routes 200 and 201 but could be found on other Dart routes from Merton. DPL8 (M208EGF) is captured by the camera at New Malden whilst on the 265. *Ian Armstrong Collection*

General, 294 new Pointer Dart SLFs were purchased, and a further eight second-hand Pointer Darts were acquired by the Company.

London General was first to take delivery of the type, with seventeen 9.2m single-doored saloons entering service from Sutton and Merton garages. LDP1 to LDP9 (P501-9RYM) were taken into stock by Sutton in November 1996 for use on route 80 (Belmont-Hackbridge), replacing MCW Metrobuses. In 2003, route 80 was again double-decked using Volvo Olympians, the Dart SLFs moving across to London Central at Bexleyheath. LDP10-7 (P510-7RYM) were new to Merton in November for route 152 (Pollards Hill-New Malden), displacing MetroRiders. Merton's allocation transferred to Peckham in March 2001 where they were put to use on the P12 between Peckham and Brockley Rise.

Twenty-seven of the type were delivered in November, again being split between Sutton and Merton. These were longer 10.0m single-doored Pointer Darts. They were predominantly used on routes 151 (Wallington-Worcester Park Station), 163 (Wimbledon Station-Morden Station) and 164 (Wimbledon Station-Sutton Station), although they were used on other services. They took up stock numbers LDP18 to LDP44 (P718-44RYL). LDP18-25 were allocated to Sutton, the others to Merton. They remained in mainstream London service until 2004 and 2005, but the lack of wheelchair ramp meant they became unsuitable for London operation. After this time, they were either used on contract work or transferred within the Go-Ahead group.

Forty-three Pointer bodied Dart SLFs were ordered for 1997 delivery, all being allocated to London Central.

Fleet numbers LDP45 to LDP89 were given to the batch which carried registration marks R445-89LGH, there was, however, no LDP50. LDP45 to LDP71 were split between New Cross and Camberwell where they displaced Leyland Titans on

The first nine LDP class Pointer Dart SLFs were allocated to Sutton for use on the 80. LDP5 (P505RYM) is seen loading at Sutton whilst heading towards Hackbridge. *Ian Armstrong Collection*

route 345 (South Kensington Station-Peckham), this service being operated by both garages. In November, a new route was introduced covering the eastern section of the 21. The 321 ran between New Cross and Sidcup and was again operated by two garages, this time shared between New Cross and Bexleyheath. The latter garage took delivery of LDP72 to LDP89. By mid-2000, the batch had been fitted with wheelchair ramps.

A handful of the Wrightbus Handybus bodied Darts inherited by London General were carrying cherished registration marks from Routemasters. These were lost in July 1998, but instead of regaining their original Northern Irish registrations they were allocated new registration marks. DW45 (545CLT) became G554SGT; DW46 (WLT346) reverted to G552SGT. DW47 lost registration WLT470 in favour of G560SGT. G551SGT was allocated to DW48, which lost WLT548. The final pair, DW52 (352CLT) and DW66 (166CLT), were re-registered to G570SGT and H881BGN respectively.

Delivery of new Plaxton Pointer bodied Dennis Dart SLFs resumed in December 1998 when twenty-seven arrived with London General. The 10.1m long saloons took up stock numbers LDP90-9, 101-28. These were the first to feature dual-doors and fitted wheelchair ramps. Registration marks WLT990, S91-8EGK, WLT599, S101-10EGK, WLT311, S112-7EGK were carried by these vehicles, all of which were allocated to Merton. They entered service in the spring of 1999 on the 155 between Elephant & Castle and Tooting, St George Hospital and the 355 (Mitcham-Brixton Station). They replaced DW class Darts and MCW Metrobuses on these services.

A new body style was introduced to the Go-Ahead London fleet in 1999. Fifteen Marshall Capital bodied Dart SLFs were delivered in May. The first five were allocated to London General. DMS1-5 (T101-5AGP) were allocated to Putney for use on the 239 (Victoria Station-Clapham Junction), and soon saw service on the 265 (Putney Bridge

Deliveries of Plaxton Pointer bodied Dennis Dart SLFs resumed in June 1999, with eleven being allocated to London General's Merton garage where they were used on the 219. LDP120 (T120KGP) represents this batch. It is seen passing through Morden. *Ian Armstrong Collection*

Station-Putney). At the same time, the other ten (DMS6-15 T106-10AGP, 101CLT, T112-5AGP) were allocated to London Central's Bexleyheath garage. They were used on the B15 (Eltham Station-Bexley) and B16 (Kidbrooke Station-Bexleyheath Station). Those allocated to Putney moved to Merton in March 2000, joining LDPs on the 152 (Pollards Hill-New Malden). They operated this route for two years before moving to London Central, where they were allocated to New Cross. They were used on the 278 (Lewisham-Ferrier Estate) and 321 (New Cross Gate-Foots Cray). DMS11 carried cherished registration 101CLT from new. In December 2002 it was re-registered T272RMY. The first DMSs left the fleet in February 2004 when the first four moved on to Go North East. Those allocated to Bexleyheath remained in use until 2009 when they were sold.

Twenty-nine 9.3m Marshall Capital bodied Dart SLFs arrived in May. They were allocated to Bexleyheath, which is where they operated until withdrawal. DML1 to DML29 (T401-11, 512, 413-9, 392, 421-9AGP) were used on B11, B12, B15, B16, 244, 469 and 401. Little happened to this batch during their time with Go-Ahead London. In 2003, DML7 transferred to Go North East for evaluation, being joined by DML9, 13, 16 and 21-9 in the spring of 2005. The other members of the batch remained in service until their ten-year lease expired in 2009.

Merton took delivery of eleven Plaxton Pointer bodied Dart SLFs in June 1999. LDP118-128 (T118-20KGP, T521AGP, T122KGP, T523AGP, T124-8KGP) were put to use on the 219 between Clapham Junction and Wimbledon. They again displaced DW class step-entrance Darts. They operated the route until 2011 when they were replaced.

1999 saw a break from the Plaxton Pointer body style, when forty-four Marshall Capital bodied Dennis Dart SLF saloons arrived with Go-Ahead London. All but five were allocated to London Central. DMS1-5 were allocated to Putney for use on the 239. DMS2 (T102KGP) is seen at Putney Bridge whilst operating route 265. *Ian Armstrong Collection*

A number of routes in the Bexleyheath area were converted to the Marshall Capital bodied Dennis Dart SLF. Twenty-nine longer DML class Dart SLFs arrived with London Central in May 1999. DML6 (T406AGP) is seen on layover at Bexleyheath town centre, whilst operating the 469. *David Beddall*

DR46 (46CLT) was re-registered back to its original mark, H546XGK, in April 2001.

A gap of almost two years passed before the next Dart SLFs arrived. Five 8.8m long Pointer MPDs were taken into stock during April 2001. Numbered LDP129 to LDP133 (Y829, 803, 831-3TGH) they were allocated to Putney for use on the 424 (West Fulham-Putney Heath). They operated on the route until June 2011, when they were returned off lease.

Eight 10.7m long Plaxton Pointer bodied Dennis Dart SLFs were allocated to Stockwell. These were numbered LDP134 to LDP141 (Y834-41TGH) and entered service on the 345, displacing older single-doored Dart SLFs. These worked alongside the Camberwell allocation until the route was converted to double-deck in 2002. After this time, they transferred to Merton for use on the 155.

Eleven shorter 8.8m MPDs were due for delivery in March 2001 but were stored by Plaxton in Scarborough until they were needed. LDP142 to LDP152 (Y842-9, 805, 851/2TGH) were delivered to Camberwell in September 2001, entering service on the C10 between Victoria Station and Elephant & Castle, taken over from Blue Triangle. They were returned off-lease in April 2011.

Thirty-eight MPDs were also taken into stock by London Central between March and May 2001. The batch was numbered LDP153 to LDP190 (Y853/4, 705, 856-9, 806, 861-6, 967-9, 907, 971-9, 908, 981-9, 909TGH). LDP153 to LDP166 were allocated to Camberwell, where they replaced DEL class Darts on the 484. Peckham took stock of LDP167 to LDP181 from where they were used on the P13 (Surrey Quays-Peckham-Streatham Garage), replacing DRLs and StarRiders in April. At the same time LDP182 to LDP190 were allocated to Camberwell for use on the P5 (Elephant & Castle-Stockwell Station), replacing DR class Darts.

The late arrival of new rolling stock at Mitcham Belle for the K5 meant that four Pointer bodied Darts were placed on loan to them from London General. The vehicles concerned were numbered DR41, 45, 51 and 52. They went on loan at the end of June 2001, returning in September.

September 2001 saw the arrival of eleven short 8.8m Pointer MPD bodied Dart SLFs at Camberwell for route C10. The batch was due to be delivered in March 2001 but were delayed. LDP147 (Y847TGH) is seen passing Pimlico School bound for Victoria. *Ian Armstrong Collection*

In March and April 2002, twenty 10.1m Plaxton Pointer bodied Dennis Dart SLFs were delivered. Rolling stock numbers LDP191 to LDP210 were allotted to this batch which was registered SN51UAD-H/J-M/O/P/R-V/X-Z. They were split between routes 80, 151, 163 and 413. LDP191-6 were allocated to Merton whilst Sutton took delivery of LDP196-210.

In November and December 2002, eleven LDPs (211-221) arrived at Stockwell. They were split between routes 170 and 239. Registration marks SK52MMU/V/X, MOA/F/U/V, MPE/F/O, MLU were carried. These were followed by LDP222-236 (SK52MLV/X-Z, MMA/E/F/J/O, MKX/Z, MRU/V/X/Y), which were also allocated to Stockwell. They were due for delivery in December 2002 but were placed into storage in Lancashire and Scotland for almost a year before entering service. LDP222-237 were eventually delivered in June 2003 and were pressed into service on the 239. They transferred to Putney between December 2003 and January 2004 where they were used to replace DR class Darts on the 39.

Stockwell and Merton took delivery of the next batch in December 2003. They were numbered LDP238 to LDP262 (SN53ETT-V/X-Z, EUA-E, KKF/G/H/J/L/M/O/P/R/T-X). LDP238-248 were allocated to Stockwell where they replaced DRL class Darts on the 239 (Victoria-Clapham Junction). LDP249-262 were allocated to Merton and used on the 355.

LDP263 to LDP272 (LX05EYP-W/Y/Z, EYA) put in an appearance during April 2005. They were allocated to Stockwell and used on the 322 between Crystal Palace and Clapham Common, the route being taken over from Travel London.

Another year passed before any more Plaxton Pointer bodied Dennis Dart SLFs were taken into stock. LDP273 to LDP280 were further 10.1m examples, these being registered LX06EYT-W, FBD/E, FAA/F/J/K/M. These were used on the 225 after the contract was renewed. They were joined by LDP281 to LDP286 (LX06FAJ/K/M/O/U,

Stockwell received eleven Pointer Darts in November and December 2002 for use on the 170 and 239. LDP218 (SK52MPE) was one of this batch and is seen passing Victoria Station whilst heading towards Clapham Junction on the 239. *Ian Armstrong Collection*

FBA), which also arrived in March 2006. The latter batch allowed the C10 to be extended to Canada Water. Both batches were allocated to New Cross.

Five additional LDPs followed in April 2006, being allocated to Stockwell. They took up numbers LDP287 to LP291 (LX06FBB/C, EZU-W) and were put to use on the 315 (Balham Station-West Norwood). The final trio of Pointer Darts arrived in May. Allocated to Putney, they were used on the 485 between Wandsworth and Richmond bus station. LDP292 to LDP294 were the fleet numbers allocated to the batch which carried registrations LX06EZZ, EZJ and EZK. In January 2007, the route and buses were transferred to the new Plough Lane garage.

September 2006 was when the takeover of Docklands Buses was completed. Eight MCV Evolution bodied ADL Darts were acquired from the fleet, along with twelve Caetano Nimbus bodied Dart SLFs, registered HV02OZS-U/W/X, PCO/U/X-Z, PDK/O. The Evolutions were numbered ED1 to ED8 (AE06HZA/C/D/F/G/H/J/K). These were used on the 368 (Harts Lane Estate-Chadwell Heath). Nine similar vehicles had been ordered by Docklands, and the order was taken on by Go-Ahead London. They duly arrived in December 2006 and followed on from the other batch, being numbered ED9 to ED17. They carried registration marks AE56OUH/J-P/S. These vehicles were allocated to route W19 (Walthamstow-Leyton-Ilford High Road). Caetano Nimbus bodied Dart SLFs were replaced in May 2007 on the 167 by a fleet of MCV Evolution bodied ADL Enviro 200 saloons (ED18-28).

Blue Triangle operations was acquired by the Company in June 2007. Twenty-one Transbus Pointer bodied Darts were transferred to the Go-Ahead London operation. DP189-209 (EJ52WXC-F, PXY/Z, PYA/B/D/F/G/H/J/L/O/P, BT04BUS, EU04BVD/F, SN56AYC/D). Some were allocated to Camberwell and New Cross for routes 108 and 360. In 2010 DP192-205 were sent to Plymouth Citybus for a refurbishment, before returning to Stockwell where they were used on the 170.

Putney received the final three new Pointer Darts purchased by Go-Ahead London. LDP294 (LX06EZK) was used on the 485. It is photographed at Hammersmith bus station. *David Beddall*

The Enviro 200 saloon replaced the Dart SLF, and this type was taken into stock by the Go-Ahead London group. However, in November 2009 eight Plaxton Pointer bodied Dennis Dart SLFs were taken into stock for use on a shuttle between Stratford International Station and Stratford Interchange. These vehicles took up stock numbers LPD295 to LDP302 (R151, 124, 146, 140, 147, 126, 142, 153RLY), originating with Metroline. LDP295-300 were allocated to Silvertown, whilst LDP301/2 were allocated to New Cross.

Go-Ahead London took over the Northumberland Park garage of First London in March 2012. At this time, a solitary Marshall Capital bodied Dart SLF was taken into stock numbered DMN1 (LT02NUK). Just over a year later, in June 2013, First withdrew from London altogether. Go-Ahead London took control of some services, garages and buses in east London. Included in this was the 193 which was operated by seventeen Marshall Capital bodied Dart SLFs. These were numbered DMN2 to DMN18 (LN51DML/M/O/P/U, LT02NUM/O/P/U/V, NVE-H/J, NUW/X). They were allocated to the former Blue Triangle garage at Rainham. These wore both the former First London fleet numbers, as well as the new ones allocated by Go-Ahead London. The 193 was taken over on 22 June 2013, the DMNs continuing to operate the route until 2017 when the route was lost to Stagecoach London.

The London operations of Metrobus were officially added to the main Go-Ahead London operation on 1 July 2014, retaining the Metrobus fleet name. From this date, several Dennis Dart SLFs transferred along with the services. The vehicles concerned were 210-6, 219, 228-236, 251-6, 271-86 and 334. Registrations for these vehicles can be found under the Metrobus heading earlier in this book.

One of two London independents to be purchased by the Go-Ahead group was Blue Triangle, this taking place in June 2007. A batch of twenty-one Pointer Darts was included in the sale and were used by their new owners on the 108, 170 and 360. DP200 (EU53PYH) is seen at Victoria whilst operating the 170. *Liam Farrer-Beddall*

Go-Ahead London's commercial department won the contract for a service between Stratford main line station and Stratford International, a route that ran through the Olympic Park site which was not open to the public at that time. For this, eight Pointer Darts were acquired from Ensign, previously operated by Metroline. LDP301 (R142RLY) represents this batch. *David Moth*

Seventeen additional Marshall Capital bodied Dennis Dart SLFs were transferred to Go-Ahead London from First London in June 2013 along with route 193, being added to the Blue Triangle operation. DMN15 (LT02NVH) is seen at Romford Station, the 193 being one of the last Dart routes to operate in London. *Liam Farrer-Beddall*

COWIE LONDON/ ARRIVA LONDON

The Cowie Group purchased two of the former London Buses Limited operations, Leaside Buses and South London. Cowie also owned Grey Green which can be found as a separate section earlier in this book. Leaside was acquired on 29 September 1994, with South London following in January 1995. On 17 October 1997, the Cowie Group became Arriva, with Leaside becoming Arriva London North and South London becoming Arriva London South. They were joined by Grey Green, which was given the title Arriva London North East.

At the time of privatisation, Leaside Buses were operating a small batch of Plaxton Pointer bodied Dennis Darts from its Wood Green garage. These vehicles were numbered DRL38 to DRL52. South London was operating both the 8.5m long DR class and 9.0m long DRL class variants of the Pointer Dart. DR20 to DR31 were the shorter vehicles, whilst DRL147 to DRL158 represented the longer type, with all of these Darts operating from Norwood. In addition, thirteen Carlyle Dartline bodied Darts were also operated by South London, these being numbered DT58 to DT70.

The first orders for new vehicles were soon placed, and in October and November 1995 fourteen Pointer bodied Darts arrived with Leaside at Enfield. Numbered LDR1 to LDR14 (N671-84GUM), these were the first 9.8m long Darts to be purchased by a London operator. They were used on the 307 in north London.

These were followed by twelve shorter 9.0m Darts. South London was the recipient of this batch, which took up rolling stock numbers DRL201 to DRL212 (N701-12GUM). They arrived during December at Thornton Heath, where they displaced SR class midibuses.

1996 was a busy year for the intake of Dennis Darts into both Leaside Buses and South London. Deliveries commenced in February when seven LDR class Darts were taken into stock from Hughes-DAF. LDR15-21 (N685-91GUM) were delivered to Leaside in an all-white livery before going through the paint shop at Enfield and being given a red livery. These were allocated to Wood Green for use on the 184. The arrival of this batch led to a chain reaction of vehicle movements. Seven of the original DRLs (DRL38-44) were transferred to South London at Thornton Heath. They displaced DT58 to DT64 from this garage, the latter vehicles moving to Leaside at Enfield where they were used on the 192, in turn replacing SR class Optare StarRiders on this service.

A further eighteen LDR class Darts were delivered to South London between July and September. They were numbered LDR22 to LDR39 by the company and carried registration marks P822-39RWU. Brixton garage took these vehicles into stock and put them to use on the 319 (Sloane Square-Streatham Hill).

The first new single-decks for the Cowie London operation arrived in October and November 1995. They were used on the 307 from Ponders End garage. The batch is represented by LDR12 (N682GUM), which is seen passing the Arkley Hotel. *Ian Armstrong Collection*

These were swiftly followed by six shorter 9.0m DRL class Pointer Darts in September. This new batch took up rolling stock numbers DRL213 to DRL218 (P913-8PWW). South London was again the recipient of this batch, these being allocated to Thornton Heath where they were used on the 455.

Sixteen additional Pointer Darts arrived during the final three months of the year, all being allocated to the Leaside operation. The first six were numbered LDR40 to LDR45 (P840-5RWU) and were added to Enfield's allocation to restock the 313, although they were frequently used on other single-deck routes from that garage. The remaining ten were allocated to Wood Green to increase the capacity on the 134. They continued on from the Enfield batch, numbered LDR46 to LDR55, carrying registration marks P846-55PWW.

Four of the original DRL class were transferred to County Bus, Harlow over the turn of 1996 and 1997. DRL47 and DRL48 moved to their new owner in December 1996, joined by DRL45 and DRL46 in January 1997. DRL47/8 lasted with County Bus until September 1997, when they were returned to London, this time being allocated to South London at Croydon. DRL201 to DRL209 also left London during 1997, being re-allocated to Londonlinks in July. These returned to Arriva London in October 1999 when they regained their original fleet numbers.

It is interesting to note that in October 1997, two third-hand Carlyle Dartline bodied Darts were purchased by Arriva London South. DT132 and DT143 both arrived from Metroline and were allocated to Thornton Heath.

As mentioned above, November 1997 was when the Cowie Group relaunched itself as Arriva. The renaming brought the Grey Green operation (Arriva London

A second class of Pointer Dart was introduced in December 1995 for the 9.0m long Darts. DRL201 (N701GUM) was allocated to Thornton Heath, it is photographed in Wallington. *Ian Armstrong Collection*

North East) closer to the other two operations. At this time, seventeen Alexander ALX200 bodied Dennis Dart SLFs registered P952-968RUL (952 to 968), were operated on routes 20 and 167, these later becoming known as ADL952-68. ADL952-8 remained in use on the 167 until the route was lost to Docklands Buses in March 2002. A year later, in March 2003, the 20 gained a fleet of double-decks which replaced ADL959-968. In both instances, the ALX200s were cascaded to other Arriva operations. Alongside these low-floor Dart SLFs came a fleet of eight Plaxton Pointer bodied step-entrance Dennis Darts. These were numbered 934 to 941 and carried registration marks L934-41GYL. These were used on the 173, and in January 1998 passed to Arriva London North, operating with them until January 2000, when they left London.

The first Plaxton Pointer bodied Dart SLFs arrived with Arriva London in August 1998. Eighteen 10.1m Pointer 2s were taken into stock at Brixton for use on the 319 (Sloane Square-Brixton). Fleet numbers DDL1-18 (S301-18JUA) were the vehicles concerned. The batch operated the route until September 2001 when new Wright Cadet bodied DAF SB120s took over. After this time, the DDLs were dispatched to Croydon where they displaced step-entrance Dennis Darts.

Five Northern Counties Paladins were transferred to Arriva London North in September 1998 for continued use on the 225. They were given the new class code DRN, with DRN115-9 (L115-9YVK) being the vehicles concerned. A month later they were allocated to Arriva London North East at Barking at which time they were repainted into the Arriva London red and cream livery. Upon retendering, the 225 passed to Stagecoach London. After this, the DRNs moved to Ponders End for use on the 192 where they were joined by DRN122/4 (L122/4YVK). In 2002, new rolling stock replaced these on the 192.

The first Plaxton Pointer bodied Dart SLFs were classified DDL by Arriva London. DDL9 (S309JUA) is seen parked on the forecourt of Thornton Heath garage. *Liam Farrer-Beddall*

A new batch of Alexander ALX200 bodied Dart SLFs arrived in October, joining similar vehicles at Arriva London North East's Barking garage, originally numbered ADL969 to ADL983 (S169-83JUA), the ADL prefixes not being carried. They were used on the 78 (Shoreditch-Peckham) in November, replacing double-deckers on the route. The batch moved with the route to Ash Grove in October 2010, before transferring to Edmonton in January 2011.

3 October 1998 saw a re-organisation of Arriva's operations in London and the Home Counties. From this date, the Edmonton garage of Arriva East Herts & Essex was placed under the control of Arriva London North, with forty-seven buses transferring. Twenty-nine of these were Dennis Dart/Dart SLFs. A fleet of thirteen step-entrance Plaxton Pointer bodied Dennis Darts registered J301-13WHJ were taken into stock at this time, retaining their former County Bus fleet numbers DP301-13. They were joined by sixteen Pointer bodied Dart SLFs which also retained their former County Bus fleet numbers, DPP416 to DPP431, registered R416-31COO. This latter batch was used on the 34 between Walthamstow Central and Barnet Church.

Arriva London North took delivery of its first Alexander ALX200 bodied Dart SLF in September 1999. The 10.2m long saloon was numbered ADL1 (V701LWT). It entered service in January 2000 on route 444 (Turnpike Lane Station-Chingford Station).

A second re-organisation of Arriva's operations in London and the Home Counties took place in October 1999. The Beddington Farm garage of Arriva Croydon and North Surrey was placed under the control of Arriva London South. Again, a number of vehicles were transferred, including fifteen Dennis Darts. Four of these carried Plaxton Pointer bodies, and were registered M160-3SKR, numbered DP160-163. DS22-4 (N542-4TPK) carried East Lancs EL2000 bodies. This latter batch remained in service until December 1999, after which time it transferred to Arriva Southern Counties. The largest batch to be taken into stock comprised eight Northern Counties Paladin bodied Dennis Darts that originated with Kentish Bus. Numbered DS120-6 and DS151, these vehicles were registered L120-6/51YVK. DS121 and 123 moved north in February 2000 when they were reallocated to Edmonton. At the same time, DS120/5/6 left London, finding a new home with Arriva North West.

Fifteen ALX200 bodied Dart SLFs arrived in November and December 1999. ADL9 to ADL23 (V609-23LGC) were longer 10.8m models. They were used on the 407 (Sutton-West Croydon-Caterham Station). They were allocated to the former Arriva Croydon & North Surrey garage at Beddington Farm. These vehicles remained in use, mainly on the 407, until the route was lost to Abellio London in October 2009, after which time the batch went north to Arriva Scotland West.

February 2000 was when a fourth class of Dart SLF for Arriva London, the PDL, was introduced. It was at this time that Arriva London North took delivery of fifteen 8.8m Pointer MPDs for use on the W15 between Hackney Central and Cogan Avenue Estate, replacing minibuses on the route. The batch took up rolling stock numbers PDL1 to PDL15 and were registered V421-435DGT. They were allocated to Edmonton garage. Two members of the batch, PDL3 and PDL15, had their identities mixed up at the time of delivery which was later rectified. They remained on the W15 until 2005 when it was replaced by larger dual-doored PDLs. They remained at Edmonton until 2008, after which time the first five moved around Arriva London as required, covering for the fitment of ibus equipment.

They were followed in March by three more MPDs (PDL16 to PDL18 W136-8VGJ). The trio was allocated to Clapton and used on the DHSS shuttle between Whitehall

The loss of the 225 saw the DRNs transfer to Enfield for the 192. DRN124 (L124YVK) was one of two extras transferred to complete the conversion of the route. It is seen at Edmonton Green whilst loading for its journey to Tottenham Hale. *Ian Armstrong Collection*

October 1998 saw the arrival of fifteen ALX200 bodied Dennis Dart SLFs with Arriva London North East for use on the 78. ADL983 (S133JUA) represents the batch. It is seen on layover at Aldgate bus station. *David Beddall*

ADL1 (V701LWT) was the first new Alexander ALX200 bodied Dart SLF to be purchased by Arriva London, arriving in September 1999. It is seen approaching Turnpike Lane Station on route 444. *Collin Lloyd/Jeff Lloyd Collection*

PDL15 (V435DGT) was one of fifteen 8.8m long Pointer MPD bodied Dart SLF saloons purchased by Arriva London to convert route W15 to the type. In 2005 they were replaced by larger Dart SLFs, with two (PDL14/15) transferring to Tottenham in November of that year. PDL15 is seen after transfer, about to pass Turnpike Lane whilst operating route W4. *Liam Farrer-Beddall*

and Elephant & Castle, replacing MR class MetroRiders on the service. These vehicles were painted into a green and blue livery for the service. In October 2005, PDL16 was repainted red and transferred to Enfield for further use. The other two moved across to Tottenham in January 2006, lasting on the contract until June of the same year at which point Arriva's involvement in the contract ceased.

ADL1 was joined on the 444 by seven more 10.2m long ALX200 bodied Dart SLFs in April 2000 when ADL2-8 were taken into stock. These vehicles carried registration marks W602-8VGJ and remained in service with Arriva London North until August 2009, at which time they joined other ADLs in Scotland.

A month later, nineteen shorter 9.4m dual-doored ALX200 bodied Dart SLFs were transferred from Arriva East Herts & Essex after control of Harlow's outstation at Debden passed to Arriva London North. These vehicles took up rolling stock numbers ADL61-9, 71-9 and 81 (W461-9, 471-9, 481XKX). At the time of transfer, they were wearing the Arriva turquoise and cream livery. They were used on routes W13 (Leytonstone-Woodford Wells) and W14 (Leyton-Woodford Bridge). Debden outstation was closed in March 2005, these ADLs moved to Edmonton. They were given a full repaint into all-over red at this time.

Twenty longer 10.7m Pointer Dart SLFs numbered PDL19 to PDL38 (X519, 471, 521-4, 475, 526/7, 478, 529, 481, 531-4, 485, 536-8GGO) joined the fleet in November and December 2000. PDL19-28 were allocated to Arriva London South at Beddington Farm where they were used on the 289 between Purley, Croydon and Elmers End. PDL29-38 found homes with Arriva London North East at Barking. These were mostly found operating the 173 between Goodmayes and Beckton Asda and could also be found on the 66 on Sundays.

Tottenham took delivery of their first PDLs in January and February 2001. These came in the form of eleven 8.8m MPDs numbered PDL39 to PDL49 (X239PGT, X541GGO, X241-4PGT, X546GGO, X246-9PGT). They were put to use on the W4 (Ferry Lane Estate-Oakthorpe Park).

In April 2001, ADL1 (V701LWT) moved to Arriva London North East at Barking. At this time, it was renumbered ADL701 to fit in with the native Dart SLFs. Between this time and September 2009 it was transferred on a number of occasions between Barking and Edmonton.

Between September and November 2001, twenty additional MPDs were taken into stock. PDL50 to PDL59 (LJ51DAA/O/U, DBO/U/V/X/Y/Z, DCE) were allocated to Thornton Heath where they were put to use on the 450 (Lower Sydenham-West Croydon). A smaller batch of four (PDL60-63 LJ51DCF/O/U/V) was allocated to Edmonton upon their arrival in October. These were used on the 377 between Ponders End and Oakwood Station. The final batch of the twenty was allocated to Ponders End for use on the 491 (Waltham Cross-North Middlesex Hospital). The vehicles concerned were numbered PDL64 to PDL69 and were registered LJ51DCX/Y/Z, DDA/E/F.

It was not until August 2002 that the next batch of MPDs was taken into stock by Arriva London. A solitary example numbered PDL70 (LF02PTZ) was added to Edmonton's allocation. At the same time, Beddington Farm benefited from the arrival of PDL71 to PDL81 (LF52UOG/H/J-P/R, UNV). These were used on the 455 (Wallington-Old Lodge Lane). PDL78-81 were delivered to the Company during September.

Thirteen MPDs arrived at Ponders End in October and November 2002 for use on the 192 (Enfield Town-Tottenham Hale Station). Rolling stock numbers

PDL55 (LJ51DBV) was part of a batch of ten Pointer MPDs taken into stock to convert route 450 to Dart SLF. It is seen at West Croydon heading towards Lower Sydenham. *Ian Armstrong Collection*

PDL82 to PDL94 were allocated to the batch which was registered LF52URY/Z, USB-D/G/H/J/L/N/O/P/R.

The arrival of these new vehicles meant that DRN118/9/22/4 were stood down. Some moved to Beddington Farm for storage, whilst a couple remained at Ponders End. There was a shortage of Darts at Beddington Farm in the summer of 2003, leading to DRN115 entering service from that garage, being transferred south from Ponders End, with DRN122 also being reinstated at this time. Also, by this time, DRN118 had transferred to Arriva the Shires, only to return to Arriva London South for a short period, being used on the 455. In October, DRN116 made the journey south. The arrival of new rolling stock at Beddington Farm led to the eventual withdrawal of the type.

DDL16-18 (S316-8JUA) moved across to Barking in the latter part of 2002 where they worked alongside PDLs on the 173, helping to cover an increase in the PVR of the route. The trio moved across to Edmonton in September 2006, before returning south to Thornton Heath in March 2007. In September 2008, DDL18 moved back to Croydon, joined by DDL16 in September 2009. The rest moved to Thornton Heath where they took over service 255 (Streatham Hill-Pollards Hill). They stayed on this route until early 2007, at which point they were mixed in with other types on the 289 (Elmers End Green-Purley Way). By the spring of 2009 the DDLs had been made redundant. Some were retained as driver trainers, whilst others left the fleet.

By 2005 Edmonton's route W15 was in need of larger vehicles. Twenty-two 9.3m long Pointer Darts were delivered to Arriva London North in February. Numbered PDL95 to PDL116, these vehicles took up registrations LJ54BCX, BAA/O/U/V, BBE/F/K/N/O/U, LHF/G/H/K-P/R, LGV. Most remained at Edmonton until 2011, although a couple were redeployed elsewhere before this. The largest move was in the opening months of 2011 when PDL101-9 transferred to Ash Grove for use on the W6.

Longer Dart SLFs were also required at Croydon in the summer of 2005. In August, seven 10.1m long Pointers were allocated to Croydon for use on the 312 between Norwood Junction and South Croydon. At this time the Norwood Junction to Peckham section of the service was withdrawn. The batch took fleet numbers PDL117 to PDL123 (LJ05GOP/U/X, GPF/K/O/U).

The final new batch of Pointer Dart SLFs to be purchased by Arriva London was allocated to Thornton Heath in September 2006. PDL124-136 (LJ56APZ, ARF/O/U/X/Z, ASO/U/V/X, AOW/X/Y) were put to use on the 450, replacing MPDs which were used as floats whilst other Dart SLFs in the fleet underwent refurbishment. In March 2007, the 450 was transferred to Beddington Farm, the Dart SLFs moving with the route. Once at Beddington, they also saw service on other Dart routes from that garage.

ADL61-3 transferred to Ponders End in March 2007 for use on the 491. In October, the trio moved south to Beddington Farm after new rolling stock took over the 491. At the same time ADL64 also moved to Beddington Farm, joined by ADL65 in November.

In early 2011, Arriva Kent Thameside lost route 162 to Metrobus. The batch of MPDs employed on that route was made redundant. In April, the batch moved to Arriva London North. They took up stock numbers PDL137 to PDL145 with their new owners. They carried registration marks SN06BPE/F/K/U/V/X-Z, BRF. PDL138 and PDL140 were temporarily allocated to Beddington Farm for use on the 455. PDL137-9 settled down at Lea Valley, whilst PDL140-5 were allocated to Ponders End.

The last new Pointer Darts were delivered to Thornton Heath in September 2006 for use on the 450. PDL130 (LJ56ASO) is seen passing through Crystal Palace on its way to West Croydon. *Liam Farrer-Beddall*

Nine Pointer MPDs new to Arriva Kent Thameside were reallocated to Arriva London in 2011 following the loss of route 162 in south-east London. PDL142 (SN06BPX) was one of six of the batch to be allocated to Ponders End. It is seen on layover at Edmonton Green bus station working route W6. *Liam Farrer-Beddall*

Arriva London lost the contract for the 462 in March 2012 to Go-Ahead London. The latter operator had ordered a batch of Wrightbus Streetlite WFs for the service. These were late arriving which led to the loan of PDL52 to PDL61 to Go-Ahead London for a short while.

The 192 was another route lost to Go-Ahead London, this time in March 2015. Again, Go-Ahead London had ordered a fleet of Wrightbus Streetlites to take over the service, and like those ordered for the 462, they were late in arriving. To cover, Arriva London lent PDL90 and PDL137-9 until March.

The London operations of Arriva the Shires at Garston and Arriva Southern Counties at Dartford and Grays were transferred to the control of Arriva London in January 2016. This led to the transfer of a number of buses to Arriva London. Included in this was a pair of ADL Pointer bodied Darts registered SN56AXG/H. They took up fleet numbers PDL150 and PDL151 respectively. Alongside these vehicles, eight PDLs were returned to Arriva London, having been cascaded to these two operators. PDL117 and PDL118 (LJ05GOP/U) returned from Arriva the Shires, whilst PDL95 and 96 (LJ54BCX, BAA) and PDL137 and PDL138 (SN06BPE/F) returned from Southern Counties. They all regained their former Arriva London numbers.

Between June and September 2020, the majority of Darts had been withdrawn and placed into store. They remained on the books of Arriva London until the summer of 2021 when they were sold by the company.

METROLINE

Metroline was privatised on 7 October 1994 and from this date a large number of Dennis Darts transferred to this new owner, these being made up of two body styles, the Plaxton Pointer and Carlyle Dartline. The Pointer Darts taken into stock were numbered DR15-9, 40/2, 81-8 and 142-8. The Carlyle Dartline dominated the single-deck fleet. DT87-143 and DT156/7 were taken into stock, all of which eventually gained the deep dark blue skirt livery.

In addition to these, a small batch of longer 9.8m Pointer Darts had been ordered by London Buses Limited, the order passing on to Metroline. Therefore, these were the first new vehicles to be taken into stock by Metroline. Taking up rolling stock numbers EDR1 to EDR9, they were registered M101-9BLE. They were allocated to Edgware from where they operated route 107 between Edgware and Barnet via Borehamwood.

Like other privatised operators, very little of interest took place concerning the Dart fleet during 1995. However, in October DT91-3, 103/8, 117/9 and 120 were made redundant at Willesden. They subsequently moved across to Edgware for further use.

EDR1 (M101BLE) was the first of forty-four Pointer Darts of this class operated by Metroline. It is seen on layover at Edgware Station. *Collin Lloyd/Jeff Lloyd Collection*

It wasn't until July 1996 that any more Darts entered the Metroline fleet. These were further examples of the 9.8m Plaxton Pointer model. Continuing from the previous batch, they took fleet numbers EDR10 to EDR16 (P285-91MLD). They were purchased for use on route H12 and were allocated to Harrow Weald.

These were followed by thirty-eight similar vehicles. EDR17 to EDR24 (P292-9MLD) arrived with the company during August, followed in September by EDR25 to EDR30 (P301-6MLD). These were also allocated to Harrow Weald where they displaced DT90, 121/2/5, 131/4/7/9 and 143 which moved to Edgware, allowing the withdrawal of SR class midibuses. September also saw the arrival of EDR31-7 (P307-13MLD) at Edgware. EDR38 to EDR44 (P314-20MLD) also arrived in September. They were initially allocated to Harrow Weald before transferring to Edgware.

On 23 November 1996, MTL London Northern took over the operation of route 79. However, new rolling stock that had been ordered by MTL had failed to materialise on time. Therefore, Metroline loaned DT87, 91/4-9 to MTL from this date. All but DT94 and DT98 were acquired by MTL London Northern in December 1996, the two vehicles mentioned being returned to Metroline in January 1997 and allocated to North Wembley.

The first low-floor Dart SLF saloons arrived with Metroline during May 1997; these being allocated to North Wembley. Rolling stock numbers DL1 to DL11 (P201-11OLX) were allocated to this batch which measured 10.0m. These single-doored saloons were put to use on the 90 between Feltham and Northolt Station. They were joined in August by DL12 to DL21 (R112-21RLY). Route 245 (Golders Green-Alperton) benefitted from this batch. DLs were replaced by DLDs on these routes in February 2003. Initially going into store, they were put to use in March on the 46 (Warwick Avenue Station-Farringdon Station). Further changes came in September 2004 when DL1-5 transferred to Potters Bar, and DL13-9 to Holloway; at the latter garage they replaced DMS and DLS class Dart SLFs on the 214. By 2005, the batch had started to leave London.

Seven shorter 9.2m Pointer Dart SLFs were purchased by Metroline, arriving with the company in June 1997. Numbered DLS1-7 (P101-7OLX), they joined the DL class saloons at North Wembley, remaining there until June 2002. The batch was mostly used on the 206 between Kilburn Park Station and St Raphael's. After being displaced from this service by new rolling stock, they transferred north to Potters Bar where they saw further service on the 383. However, they did not last long there, as in May 2003 they moved to Holloway for use on the 214, a route which was experiencing length restrictions at this time. This was resolved in February 2004, and they were retained at Holloway until September, after which time they were shared between Potters Bar, North Wembley and Perivale. They finally left London in 2005.

The first sizable batch of Pointer bodied Dart SLFs arrived over the course of September and October 1997 at Cricklewood. Thirty-two 10.0m long examples arrived, introducing a third classification code for the low-floor Dart SLF. DLD22 to DLD53 (R122-53RLY) were put to use on two new services, the 189 (Kilburn-Cricklewood-Brent Cross) and 316 (North Kensington-Cricklewood-Neasden). Arriving early, these vehicles initially saw service on the 113. The 316 was lost to F.E. Thorpe in October 2002, with the batch being used on the 16 after this time. In March 1998, the 189 was extended to Oxford Circus, and in February 2003 double-deckers took over the service. This latter conversion led to the transfer of the majority of this batch across to North Wembley, where they replaced the DL class Dart SLFs mentioned above.

The introduction of Dart SLFs saw the withdrawal of the first DT class Darts at the end of 1996. Those allocated to North Wembley were the first to go. After this cull, nineteen DT class Darts remained in service with the Company. From this first wave of withdrawals, it is notable that DT132 and DT143 were sold to Arriva London South in October 1997.

Three DT class Darts were repainted in an all-over blue livery for use on various Tesco contracts in North London in 1997. First to be completed was DT89, which received the livery in January, followed by DT93 in February, whilst DT100 changed colour during May.

The next batch of 10.1m Dart SLFs arrived in the summer of 1998, again carrying Plaxton Pointer bodywork. R154-63VLA arrived at Cricklewood numbered DLD54 to DLD63 in May and June. They were put to use on the 143 between Archway Station and Hendon Central Station, also seeing service on the 302. The 143 moved across to Holloway in March 2000, but the DLDs remained at Cricklewood, initially being used on the 232 between Wood Green and St Raphael's Estate. In May 2000, they transferred to Holloway where they were put back on the 143. They were swapped for DLD108-117 which had wheelchair ramps fitted, unlike DLD54-63.

June also saw the arrival of eleven DLDs at Willesden. DLD64-74 (R164-74VLA) were used on the 302 (Mill Hill Broadway-Kensal Rise). Route 297 moved from Willesden to Perivale in June 2003, and this batch of DLDs moved across with it. The batch soon went on a three-month loan to Potters Bar for use on the W8, the 297 being converted to double-deck operation in their absence. Returning to Perivale in September 2003, they soon left again after the 297 was permanently converted to double-deck operation

May 1997 saw the arrival of the first low-floor Dart SLFs with Metroline. DL1 (P201OLX) is seen loading at Hatton Cross bus station whilst operating route 90 to nearby Feltham. *Ian Armstrong Collection*

The DLS class totalled just seven with Metroline, these being shorter 9.3m Pointer Dart SLFs. They were originally allocated to North Wembley for use on the 206. The batch is represented by DLS5 (P105OLX). *Ian Armstrong Collection*

DLD24 (R124RLY) represents the thirty-two strong batch of Pointer Dart SLFs purchased to take over routes 113, 189 and 316 in the latter part of 1997. It is seen at Brent Cross on route 189, heading into Central London. *Ian Armstrong Collection*

in December. Some of the batch went on to replace EDR class step-entrance Darts, while others were retained for use on the 112. DLD67-70 moved to Edgware, whilst DLD73 found a new home at Cricklewood. These vehicles continued to be used around Metroline as required until 2008/2009 when they left the fleet.

A third batch arrived in June in the form of eleven 10.1m saloons. DL75-85 were allocated to North Wembley and put to use on the 245 (Golders Green-Alperton). Registered R175-85VLA, they were joined by the earlier DL class Dart SLFs on this route, and also saw service on the 90. In early 2003, DL76-85 moved to Potters Bar to replace DMS and DLS class Dart SLFs from the 234, 326 and 383. The 326 was transferred from Potters Bar to Cricklewood in July 2003, and DL76-85 moved with the route. A shuffle of Dart SLFs in 2004 meant that this batch transferred to Holloway for use on the 214. They lasted there until late 2005, after which time they were withdrawn and sold.

Metroline took over the business of MTL London Northern in August 1998. This brought with it a number of step-entrance and low-floor Darts. The step-entrance Darts carried Plaxton Pointer bodies and were numbered DRL17 to DRL37. A small number of DP class Darts originating with both R&I Tours and London Northern themselves were also acquired. They retained fleet numbers DP233/4/6-42 (J823GGF, K414/6/7/8/9MGN, RIB8431), as well as EDR45-8 M498/9, 503-6ALP. DP273-6 were also taken into stock, these carrying registration marks P273-6MLE. A second batch of DPs, originating with Thamesway, were also taken into stock. These were numbered DP901 to DP917 and carried registration marks K901-17CVW. This batch soon left Metroline, going to either First Capital or First Essex Buses for further service. Both types were allocated to Holloway from where they were shared between routes 46 (Kensal Rise Station-Farringdon) and 274 (Angel Islington-Marble Arch). Of these, DRL21 to DRL37 later moved to Potters Bar to oust the shorter DR class Darts that had been transferred there from other Metroline garages during 1999. Alongside the Plaxton Pointers, a small batch of nineteen Northern Counties Paladin bodied Dennis Darts were also acquired. DNL101-10/2-9 (L101HHV etc) were based at Holloway and used on the C2. A solitary Carlyle Dartline, DC229 (G129RGT), was also acquired.

Sixty-seven Marshall Capital bodied Dart SLFs were also acquired, divided between the 10.2m DMS class and longer 10.2m DML class. DMS1-20 (R701-11, 699MEW, S513-20KFL) were used from Potters Bar on routes 234, 326 and 384. In May 2007, DMS1-12 moved to Perivale for use on the E6 until new Enviro 200s arrived. The DML class comprised forty-seven saloons numbered DML1-47 (R681-98MEW, R619-32VEG, R863-77MCE). DML1-18 saw service from North Acton on the 139 until September 2000 when they moved to Cricklewood following the closure of North Acton. In July 2003 the batch moved to Holloway for use on the C11 (Archway Station-Cricklwood). The route moved to the former F.E. Thorpe garage in February 2005, and the batch moved between West Perivale and North Wembley as required until the summer of 2007 when they left London. DML19-32 533-5 were allocated to Potters Bar for routes from that garage including the 217. They were later renumbered DML519-532.

Fifteen 10.1m Pointer Dart SLFs arrived in December 1998 at Willesden for use on the 297 (Willesden Garage-Ealing Broadway). Stock numbers DLD86-100 (S286-99, 301JLP) were allocated to the batch. In June 2003, they were meant to transfer to Perivale along with the 297. However, they grounded when entering Perivale garage so were not suitable. DLD60-74 went in their place, with DLD86-100 staying at Willesden for the 302. They stayed true to the 302 until April 2010 when they were replaced. Some were then sold, others reallocated to Holloway, and the training fleet.

Two lengths of Marshall Capital bodied Dennis Dart SLFs were acquired from MTL London Northern. The longer of the two were classified DML. DML12 (R692MEW) is seen at Edgware bus station about to depart for Kilburn Park Station on the 32. *Ian Armstrong Collection*

The shorter Marshall bodied Dart SLFs were classified DMS. DMS21 (S521KFL) is seen parked on the forecourt of Potters Bar garage during one of the annual open days at the Hertfordshire garage. *David Beddall*

Three Marshall Capital bodied Dart SLFs were the first new Darts to enter the Metroline fleet in 1999. DML533-5 (T63-5KLD) arrived at Potters Bar in March and were used to replace MCW Metrobuses on the 317 (Enfield Town-Waltham Cross). They remained at Potters Bar until October 2007 when they were withdrawn and sold.

1999 also saw the arrival of twenty-five DLDs with Metroline. Potters Bar received the first ten for use on the 232 in July. Fleet numbers DLD108 to DLD117 were allocated to these vehicles along with registration marks T48/9, 39, 51-4, 35, 36, 47KLD. This batch measured 10.2m, slightly longer than previous DLDs.

The other fifteen arrived in September and October. DLD118 to DLD123 (V118-20, 134, 122/3GBY) were allocated to Harrow Weald for use on the H12 and H14. Edgware took delivery of the others for route 107. They were numbered DLD124-132 (V124-32GBY). DLD124 and DLD125 soon moved to Harrow Weald. After the withdrawal of the H14 in September 2004, DLD118-25 transferred to Park Royal for use on the 46. At the same time, DLD126-131 also moved across to North Wembley for use on the 46.

A white-based livery was applied to DR94 in January 2000. The vehicle was used to promote Safeway supermarkets.

The next batch of Plaxton Pointer bodied Dennis Dart SLFs did not arrive until May 2000. DLD133-149 (W133/4, 151, 136-9, 152, 141-4, 153, 146-9ULR) were allocated to Holloway where they were put to use on the C2. The conversion of the C2 to low-floor operation caused a number of transfers. The DNLs that had been operating the route were put to use on the 214 at Holloway, replacing DRL class Darts. In turn they transferred to Potters Bar for routes 383, PB1 and W4, replacing the shorter DR class Darts. Some of the DP class Darts were used on the 112 between Ealing Broadway and Brent Cross, with others working alongside DRLs on the C11 (Archway Station-Brent Cross). The DRLs did not operate the C11 for long, some soon moving across to North Wembley where they were used on the PR1 and PR2.

The final Dart SLFs to arrive in 2000 did so in December. A pair of short 8.8m MPDs arrived at Potters Bar for use on the PB1. This introduced a fourth classification code to Metroline, the DLM. The vehicles concerned were numbered DLM150/1 (X567/8LLX). Eight more followed in January 2001 numbered DLM152-160 (Y252-4, 251, 256-9, 151NLK). These were allocated to Holloway for use on the W5 (Harringay-Archway Station). In July 2003, the W5 moved to King's Cross along with the fleet of DLMs, moving back to Holloway in April 2005. They remained there until February 2011 when DLM152 and DLM158 moved to Potters Bar, the others being sold.

Route 274 (Islington-Lancaster Gate) received new rolling stock in May and June 2001. At this time fifteen 10.1m Dart SLFs were allocated to Holloway numbered DLD161 to DLD175 (Y661-5NLO, Y161NLK, Y667-9, 161, 671-5NLO). In July 2003 the batch moved to King's Cross where they saw out their days with Metroline

DLD176-183 (Y153, 237-9, 158NLK, Y659/2/3NLO) arrived in June. They were allocated to Potters Bar for route 268 (Golders Green Station-Finchley Road). In February 2002, DLD176 moved to Holloway, later transferring to King's Cross in July 2003, joining the batch above on the 274. November 2005 saw the rest of the batch transfer to North Wembley.

A third batch numbered DLD184-197 (Y654/8/6/7NLO, Y248/9, 154, 261-5, 159/7NLK) arrived in June. Allocated to Harlesden they were used on the 95 between Southall and Shepherd's Bush Green. The route and buses moved to Perivale in August 2002. Between December 2007 and February 2008, this batch migrated across to Potters Bar where they remained until withdrawal in September 2011.

A batch of eleven 8.8m long Pointer MPDs arrived in December 2000 / January 2001, with nine of them entering service on the W5. The penultimate member of the batch, DLM159 (Y259NLK), is seen on layover near Archway Station. *Ian Armstrong Collection*

The summer of 2001 saw the arrival of fifteen Plaxton Pointer bodied Dennis Dart SLF saloons for the 274, allocated to Holloway. DLD175 (Y675NLO) was the last of the batch. *Ian Armstrong Collection*

The DP class Darts inherited from London Northern remained operating from Holloway until the summer of 2001 when they were replaced on the 274 by new rolling stock. However, this did not spell the end of these vehicles in London; they were subsequently transferred to Potters Bar. DP273 to DP276 were put to use as both staff buses and driver training vehicles as the need arose. The middle two of the batch, DP274 and DP275, were used as rest rooms at the East Acton terminus of route 7, with DP274 later being used at Northolt. DP275 was sold in November 2019 to the Bromley Bus Preservation Group. The same group took DP274 in May 2021.

Eleven DLDs arrived at Edgware in February 2002 for routes 251, 288, 303 and 305. Fleet numbers DLD198 to DLD207 were given to these vehicles, which carried registration marks LN51KXD/E/F/G/H/J/L/M/O. They remained at Edgware until August 2002 at which time the 288 and 305 moved to North Wembley, the DLDs transferring with them. The winter of 2007 and 2008 was when the batch converted to driver training vehicles. They remained in this use for a number of years, being withdrawn between December 2012 and June 2013.

Yet another classification code was introduced in 2002, the DSD. These Pointer Darts measured 9.3m in length. DSD208 to DSD217 (LR02DXV/X-Z, BEJ/O/U/Y, BFA/E) were originally allocated to Harlesden for route 206. They were then reallocated to North Wembley where they remained until October 2007. It was at this time that they were replaced by MM class MAN/MCV Evolution saloons and were reallocated to Potters Bar.

Two operators were acquired by Metroline in 2004, the first acquisition taking place in August. At this time, the business and vehicles of F.E. Thorpe were acquired, bringing sixty Plaxton Pointer bodied Dennis Dart SLFs into the fleet. These were numbered DLF9 (R309NGM), DLF29-40 (S529-40JLM), DLF63-77 (W963-77TRP), DLF80-110 (KU52YLG/H, YKL/N/O/P/R/S/T/V/X/Y, YKA-H/J/K/Z, YLA-F) and DLF124/5 (KX53SDU/V). A solitary Marshall Capital bodied Dart SLF was also taken into stock, numbered MLF122 (AJ02PZY). The F.E. Thorpe operation was kept separate for a while, but eventually the vehicles received Metroline livery and fleet names. The fleet initially operated from West Perivale, where most remained for their careers with Metroline. They were used on various routes in north-west London. The majority of the batch went off lease between 2008 and 2010 when new Enviro 200 saloons were taken into stock. Some survived for a little longer, these being detailed below.

The second acquisition took place in November when the business of Armchair, Brentford was acquired along with fifty Plaxton Pointer bodied Dennis Dart SLFs. These retained their former Armchair fleet numbers, DP962, 1001-1049 (Y962KRX, RX51FNP/S/T, Y63LTF, RX51FNW/V/U/Y, RL51DOA, DNX, DOJ/H, DNY/V, DOU, DNU, KP02PUF/H/J/O, PVD/E, PUK, PVF/K/J/L/O/N/T/U, PWN, KU02YUB-D, KP02PWU/V/O, KU02YUE/J/KM KM02HFK/N/L, HFO, HGD/E/F, KX54NJO). They were all initially allocated to the former Armchair garage in Brentford, but over the years they moved about Metroline as required. Alongside these came a smaller batch of thirteen Alexander ALX200 bodied Dennis Dart SLFs used on the 209. These vehicles were numbered DA140-152 (T140-52AUA).

The southern section of the former Stationlink service, the 705, was withdrawn in May 2005. The seven single-doored DLFs (104-110) were retained by Metroline, initially being used on routes in west London. In September 2006, the batch was transferred to Potters Bar to replace the aging fleet of Volvo Olympians on the 84 between Barnet and St Albans. They remained on the route until May 2008 when new Enviro 200s took over. DLF9 (R309NGM) was also transferred to Potters Bar at this time. They ended their careers with Metroline as driver training vehicles, leaving the fleet in 2010.

The arrival of a batch of 9.3m long Pointer Dart SLFs introduced yet another class code for the type with Metroline. Route 206 received ten which they gave the DSD class code. The batch is represented by DSD209 (LR02BDX). *Ian Armstrong Collection*

Metroline lost the Stationlink service inherited from F.E. Thorpe in September 2005. The vehicles used were retained and in September 2006 they were transferred to Potters Bar. DLF109 (KU52YLE) was one of these vehicles and it is seen operating non-TfL service 84 (St Albans – New Barnet Station). It is seen on layover in St Peters Street, St Albans. *David Beddall*

Transport for London had specified that by the end of 2005 all buses operating their contracts should have fitted wheelchair ramps. A number of the DL class Dart SLFs did not meet this standard, leading to their withdrawal. This left a gap in the Metroline fleet which was filled by the addition of nineteen ADL Pointer Dart saloons. DLD693 to DLD711 (LK55KLE/F/J/L/M/O/P/S/U/V/X/Z, KMA/E/F/G/J/M/O) arrived between December 2005 and January 2006 and were added to Holloway's allocation. They were used on routes 46, 214 and 274.

Former Armchair DP962 (Y962KRX) was transferred from Brentford to Potters Bar in July 2006 where it was used on the 84, 234, 242 and W9. A couple of months later it lost its Armchair livery in favour of Metroline colours. It was operated by Potters Bar until February 2009, after which time it was sold. September 2006 was when two former F.E. Thorpe Dart SLFs (DLF82/6) transferred to North Wembley, only to return to Perivale in February 2008.

Although DLD693-711 were the last new Dart SLFs to be acquired by Metroline, a number of second-hand models were also acquired. Nineteen Pointer bodied Dart SLFs were acquired from Dawson Rentals in September 2006, these previously operating with Mitcham Belle and Centra London. They were numbered DP12, 14, 16-9, 22, 24, 26-8, 32-4, 36-8, 43/9 (W112WGT etc). They were initially allocated to F.E. Thorpe's Perivale garage before being distributed around the Metroline group.

DLD693-711 were completely refurbished by Hants and Dorset Trim in Eastleigh, returning to London in time for the London 2012 Olympic Games in July and August 2012.

The last new batch of Pointer Darts to be taken into stock by Metroline were allocated to Holloway. They originally wore a light-blue skirt before receiving the 100 per cent red livery. DLD698 (LK55KLO) is seen heading to Lancaster Gate on route 274 whilst passing through Marble Arch. *Liam Farrer-Beddall*

DC1556 (LK53FDO) represents the batch of Caetano Nimbus bodied Darts acquired from First London. It is seen departing Hayes and Harlington town centre. *Liam Farrer-Beddall*

For the duration of the games, this batch was placed under the care of Stagecoach UK Bus Events, and allocated to both West Ham and Beckton Park garages, the latter being a temporary garage for the Olympics.

Mention has already been made in the First London section that in June 2013 they sold off their London operations, with Metroline being one of three companies to acquire some of its garages and vehicles. A modest batch of twenty Caetano Nimbus bodied Darts was acquired, all being allocated to Uxbridge. At this time, the former DMC41503-11, 526, 528-537 were taken into stock and renumbered DC1540-1559 by Metroline. They continued to operate from Uxbridge garage where they remained until late 2015, early 2016 when they were sold on to Ensign. Registration marks LK03NLE-G/J/L/M/T, NFY/Z, LK53FDC/E-G/J/M-P/U/V were carried by these vehicles.

DLD693-711 were the last Dennis Dart SLFs to operate with Metroline, remaining in use from King's Cross on the 214 until November 2018 when Enviro 200s were transferred to replace them. DLD699 was the last Dart SLF to operate with the Company.

MTL LONDON NORTHERN

MTL Holdings Ltd purchased London Northern on 26 October 1994. Like the other London Buses Limited operations, a number of Dennis Darts were acquired. At the time of takeover, London Northern was operating from garages at Holloway and Potters Bar.

Shortly before privatisation London Buses Limited had received a batch of nineteen Northern Counties Paladin bodied Dennis Darts numbered DNL101-10/2-9 (L101HHV etc). These were acquired by London Northern and continued operating route C2 from Holloway. This was also the base for DRL17 to DRL37 which were also acquired by London Northern.

MTL London Northern acquired the business of R&I Buses of Acton in October 1995. With this came a number of Dennis Dart saloons. DC216/9/20 (G216/9/21LGK) carried the original Duple Dartline body style, whilst DC221/4/9 (G121/4/9RGT) had the Carlyle Dartline body. A larger fleet of Plaxton Pointer bodied Dennis Dart saloons were also acquired. They were numbered DP233/4/6-41/5-8 (J823GGF, K414/6/7/8/9MGN, M498/9, 503-6ALP). The final Dart to be acquired was a solitary Marshall bodied example registered RIB8431, numbered 242.

DC221 (G121RGT) was one of three Dennis Dart saloons inherited from R&I Buses to carry the Carlyle Dartline body style. It is seen parked on Stonecutter Street whilst operating route 46. *Ian Armstrong Collection*

London Northern took over operation of the 79 in November 1996. New vehicles had been ordered for the route, but these failed to arrive on time. Therefore, eight DT class Darts were loaned from Metroline (DT87, 91/4-9). DT94/8 returned to Metroline, the other six being acquired by the company during December. These operated alongside other Darts in the fleet on routes 46, 112 and 274.

It wasn't until May 1997 that the new rolling stock arrived. Four Plaxton Pointer bodied Darts registered P273-6MLE were delivered at this time, taking up rolling stock numbers DP273-6. These thirty-four seaters measured 9.2m in length.

Holloway took over the contract for route 214 in February 1998 from Thamesway. London Northern took DP901 to DP917 (K901-17CVW) into stock at this time, operating them until August when Metroline acquired the business. Details of the batch can be found under that heading in the previous section.

The first Dennis Dart SLF saloons arrived with London Northern in February 1998 when eleven 9.3m long single-doored Marshall C39 bodied saloons entered service from Potters Bar on the 234 between East Finchley Station and Barnet. These vehicles were numbered DMS2 to DMS12 and carried registration marks R702-11, 699MEW. DMS1 (R701MEW) followed in August, completing this batch. The next seventeen arrived in August to convert route 326 (Brent Cross-Barnet) and 384 (Cockfosters Station-Barnet) to the type. These too were allocated to Potters Bar, and took fleet

P673MLE was allotted rolling stock number DP273 by MTL London Northern when it arrived in 1997. It is seen heading towards Marble Arch on the 274. *Matthew Wharmby*

numbers DMS13 to DMS29 (S513-29KFL). DMS27-9 were the last to arrive, putting in an appearance just before the Metroline take-over.

They were joined in March 1998 by eighteen 10.2m long DML class Marshall bodied Dart SLFs. These were for use on the 139, taking the type into Central London. DML1-18 (R681-98MEW) were allocated to North Acton, displacing Routemasters on the service. A couple of months passed before the next batch arrived in May. Carrying on the numbering sequence as DML19 to DML32 (R619-32VEG), these vehicles were put to use from Potters Bar on route 217 (Turnpike Lane-Waltham Cross). They were soon numbered DML519 to DML532 to denote the single-door layout. A third batch totalling fifteen arrived in July at Holloway for use on the C11. The vehicles in question were numbered DML33-47 and carried registration marks R863-77MCE.

The services and vehicles of MTL London Northern were acquired by Metroline in August 1998, resulting in the transfer of the Dennis Darts and Dart SLF saloons mentioned above to the new owner. The sale of London Northern to Metroline meant that the other DT class Darts transferred between the two operations.

Waltham Cross bus station finds DMS3 (R703 MEW), one of twelve acquired for the conversion of route 234 to low-floor buses. It is seen off route, operating route 217. *Ian Armstrong Collection*

LONDON UNITED

London United was privatised on 5 November 1994 and was purchased by its management. The Company took a large number of Dennis Dart saloons into stock, carrying both the Plaxton Pointer and Carlyle Dartline body styles. The 8.5m long DR class Pointer Dart was heavily represented in the fleet at this time. Those operated were numbered DR1 to DR14, DR53-80 and DR99-141. They worked alongside longer 9.0m DRL class saloons numbered DRL96-108 and DRL159-171. The DRs were distributed between Fulwell, Hounslow and Shepherd's Bush outstation Wood Lane. The DRLs operated exclusively from Hounslow. The Carlyle Dartline DT class also featured heavily in the London United fleet. DT1-27/9, 41-54/6/7, 71-86, 144-55/8-68 were shared between Fulwell, Hounslow and Stamford Brook. A stylish livery of red, with white and grey, was applied to the fleet of Darts under the control of London United.

The Company was chosen to operate the Airbus routes between Heathrow Airport and Central London, these originally being operated using MCW Metrobuses. A new service commenced under the Airbus Direct brand on 15 July 1995. The service linked Heathrow with around 150 hotels in Central London. The new route was operated by thirty-five DTs (DT1-29, 41/3/5/6/7 and 168) which were converted for this use. They were re-seated from B28F to DP21F and had additional luggage racks installed. They were repainted all-red with prominent yellow Airbus Direct names and featured a red and grey interior. The work was carried out at Hants and Dorset Trim in Eastleigh. The batch was allocated to West Ramp, Heathrow and remained on the service until November 1999 when it was withdrawn. Before this DT44-7, 168 were transferred to Shepherd's Bush for further use, retaining the DP21F layout, but lost the luggage racks.

In September 1995, London United took over the operation and vehicles of Westlink from West Midlands Travel. This introduced fourteen Wrightbus Handybus bodied Dennis Darts into the fleet, these being numbered DWL1 to DWL14. Westlink was initially operated as a separate operating company, based at a garage at Hounslow Heath.

DR10-4 were transferred to Westlink in June 1996, making the short journey to Hounslow Heath from Hounslow. At the same time, DRL99-104 were transferred from Hounslow to Fulwell. DRL166 was given a blue livery for use on 555/6/7 group of services in Surrey in September 1996.

The first low-floor Dart SLFs were received by London United between September and November 1996. The batch of eight carried Wright Crusader bodywork and were numbered CD1-8. Measuring 10.2m, these vehicles carried Northern Ireland registration marks VDZ8001-8. The first members of the batch entered service on route H37 in October before taking up service on their intended service, the H25 (Hanworth-Hatton Cross). A red livery, complete with grey skirt and white roof, was

DT168 (500CLT) represents the Airbus Direct operation introduced by London United in July 1995. The fleet of Carlyle Dartline bodied Darts underwent a full refurbishment before entering service. DT168 is captured by the camera rounding Marble Arch. *Colin Lloyd/Jeff Lloyd Collection*

worn by these vehicles. In February 2000, they moved to Hounslow Heath, along with the H25. Tellings-Golden Miller won the contract for the H25 in November 2001, after which time CD1 and CD3 moved to Stamford Brook for use on the H91. At the same time, CD2/4/5/7 moved to Tolworth for use on the 371. CD6 and CD8 were retained by Hounslow for route 216. Those allocated to Tolworth moved to Stamford Brook in May 2002 for the take up of route 440 (Stamford Brook Garage-Park Royal Asda). They remained on this service until 2006 when they moved within the RATP Group to Yellow Buses in Bournemouth.

Two DT class Darts were re-registered to their original registration marks in 1997. DT75 (WLT329) and DT164 (WLT804) lost these for H575MOC and H264NON.

Although London United took delivery of the eight Wright Crusader bodied Dart SLFs in 1996, the preferred model was the Plaxton Pointer bodied Dart SLF. Unlike other London operators, London United was quite slow in taking this model into stock. The first arrived in July 1998 when six 10.6m Pointer Darts were allocated to Fulwell for route R70 (Richmond-Nurserylands). The vehicles concerned were numbered DP1 to DP11 (S301-11MKH), and carried route branding, this being applied in September. The R70, along with the R68, were lost to Tellings-Golden Miller in August 2000. After this time, Fulwell retained the first five for route 411. DP6-11 transferred to Hounslow for use on the 81 (Hounslow-Slough). A month after, DP1-5 transferred to Kingston along with the 411. The batch transferred to Hounslow in January 2001 to complete the allocation on the 406 (Kingston-Epsom).

Twenty-two longer 10.7m Pointer Darts were taken into stock by London United in February 1999, this time built to dual-door layout. DP12-22 (T412-22KAG) were painted into an orange, blue and red livery, similar to that worn by South West Trains at that time. They were used on a new Railair service linking Feltham with both Heathrow Central and Heathrow Terminal 4 on two routes. The routes were short lived, with the terminal 4 service being withdrawn in 2000. Five of the batch received

London United's first low-floor Dennis Dart SLFs carried the Wright Crusader body style. They were new to Hounslow for use on the H25, although CD1 and CD3 moved to Stamford Brook for use on the H91 in November 2001 after the H25 was lost. CD3 (VDZ8003) is seen on the H91, on layover at Hounslow West Underground station. *Ian Armstrong Collection*

DR13 (H113THE) was one of five Pointer Darts transferred to the Westlink operation in June 1996. Upon transfer they lost London United fleet names in favour of Westlink ones. DR13 is seen loading at Richmond bus station. *Ian Armstrong Collection*

The first eleven Plaxton Pointer bodied Dart SLFs were new to London United for route R70. After the loss of the route in September 2000 the DP class Dart SLFs were put to use on other services. DP3 (S303MKH) eventually settled at Hounslow garage. It is seen operating route 81 to Slough, loading on Bath Road on the edge of Heathrow Airport. *Ian Armstrong Collection*

fleet livery in July and were used on routes 81, H22, H37 and H98. The Central area service continued until November 2001, after which time it was replaced by a rerouting of the 285. These vehicles were put to use on the H23, and again received fleet livery. DP23-33 (T422-33KRG) were delivered in all-over blue for use on routes 555/6/7, these linking Heathrow Airport with surrounding villages. This batch was allocated to West Ramp, Heathrow garage. The three services were lost to Tellings-Golden Miller, with DP23-33 being used to cover an increase in PVR on other services, in June 2003.

Deliveries picked up a pace in July and August 1999, with forty-six 10.7m DP class Pointer Dart SLFs entering service in the Hounslow area. The batch was numbered DP34 to DP79 (T334-54, 455, 356-75PRH, T976-80SRH). They were shared between routes H22, H23, H37 and H98, with appearances on the 81 and H91. Thirty of the batch, DP34-63, were allocated to Hounslow, whilst DP64-79 were added to Hounslow Heath's allocation. A number of those allocated to Hounslow moved across to Hounslow Heath in October 2009, displacing shorter DPS class Pointer Darts.

Investment in this new rolling stock led to the withdrawal of a number of DT class Darts in October 1999, the last of the type leaving London in July 2000.

Further Pointer Dart SLFs arrived in October. DP81 to DP99 (V781-5, 886, 787-99FKH) were allocated to Shepherd's Bush garage for use on route 49 (Clapham Junction-Shepherd's Bush Green). They were followed in December by a batch of shorter 10.1m Pointer Dart SLFs, this type being designated the DPS classification code. V801-3, 904, 805-16KAG took up rolling stock numbers DPS1-16 and were put to use on the 72 (East Acton-Roehampton). These were again allocated to Shepherd's Bush, the two batches being the first low-floor singles to be allocated to this garage. The latter batch remained in use on the 72 until November 2007 when they were swapped with a batch from Stamford Brook.

Again, the arrival of this new rolling stock meant that a number of the older step-entrance Darts were withdrawn. DR10/3, 99, 102/7-9, 126/8, 130/6/9 and 150 were mostly used on the 72 before the arrival of the DPS class Dart SLFs. After their arrival, these DRs moved to Fulwell where they replaced DT class Darts on the 33.

Two DR class Pointer Darts lost their cherished registrations in March 2000. DR11 (WLT931) and DR100 (VLT23) regained their original registration marks H611TKU and J610DUV.

The final batch of 10.7m Pointer bodied Dart SLFs arrived with London United during September 2000. DP500-509 (X611, 601-9OKH) were allocated to Hounslow for use on the 222 between Hounslow and Uxbridge. They displaced the first generation low-floor Dennis Lance SLFs on the service. The batch was withdrawn in April 2010 and left London by the end of the year.

Eighteen shorter dual-doored DPS class Dart SLFs arrived at Fulwell in November. Fleet numbers DPS511-4/6-9, 521-4/6-9, 531-3 were allocated to these vehicles which were registered X511-4/6-9/21-4/6-9/31-3UAT. They were put to use on the 33 between Hammersmith, Twickenham and Fulwell garage. They arrived numbered DP511 etc. but were soon rectified. The gaps in the fleet numbers resulted from no matching registration marks being available. With the exception of DPS533, the batch remained at Fulwell until the 33 was lost in November 2005, after which time they moved to Hounslow Heath for the 411 and H22.

Seven months passed before the next batch of Pointer bodied Dart SLFs was taken into stock. Nineteen 10.1m Darts for use on the 285 (Kingston-Heathrow Airport) arrived in June 2001. Rolling stock numbers DPS534/6-9/41-4/6-9/51-4/6/7 were

Perhaps the smartest livery to be applied to London's Dart SLFs was the red, orange and blue livery worn by DP12 to DP22. DP15 (T415KAG) shows off this smart livery whilst parked at Feltham Station. Route T123 was later replaced by the diversion of the 285 to Feltham. *Ian Armstrong Collection*

Another eleven Dart SLFs, DP23-33, wore a blue livery for use on non-London routes 555/6/7, running between Heathrow Airport and nearby villages in Surrey. DP31 (T431KAG) is seen at Heathrow Central sporting this livery. *Ian Armstrong Collection*

At the same time a batch of sixteen shorter 10.1m long Pointer Darts were also allocated to Shepherd's Bush. They were put to use on the 72 as is demonstrated by DPS4 (V904KAG), seen heading towards East Acton. *Ian Armstrong Collection*

allocated to the batch which carried registration marks Y534/6-9/41-4/6-9/5-4/6/7XAG. They were allocated to Hounslow Heath, although only ten had been received by the time the service started on 30 June. The gap was filled by a selection of single-decks until the outstanding nine arrived, these included DP64-67. DPS552/4-7 were delivered to Shepherd's Bush for use on the 72, before moving to Hounslow Heath in August. This batch was not intended for the 285, instead they were ordered to Tolworth's routes K1 and K4 in the Kingston area, replacing step-entrance Darts.

November and December 2001 was when the intended batch of DPS class Dart SLFs for the 285 were taken into stock. DPS558-78 (SN51SZV/W-Z, SXX-Z, SXK/L/M/O/C, SZF/G/J/K/L/O/P/R) were allocated to Hounslow Heath and featured additional luggage space. Route branding was applied to the vehicles featuring a blue and white diagonal band. It was at this time that the 285 was diverted via Feltham to replace the T123.

December also saw the arrival of DPS579-602 (SN51TAU, TBY, TCV, TDV, TBO, TCJ/Y, TDZ, TBU, TCK/Z, TEJ, TBV, TCO, TDO, TEO, TBX, TCU, TDU and TEU). DPS579 to DPS586 were allocated to Fulwell for use on the 290, replacing DR class step entrance Dennis Darts. DPS587 to DPS602 were allocated to Tolworth for route 371, replacing the fleet of Optare Excels and MAN Vectras. DPS587-92/5/6/9 transferred to Fulwell in April 2007 after part of Tolworth's parking space was acquired by Network Rail. They retained the same set of blinds which restricted their use to the 371, 406 or 418.

Thirteen 8.8m long MPDs were delivered in between these two batches, arriving at Tolworth in November. DPK603-615 (SN51SXP/R-W, SXD-H/J) were used on routes K2 and K3 in the Kingston area. The DPS class code was already in use by London United, so the company decided to allocate the DPK classification code to the type, the K standing for Kingston. They operated the services until July 2008, after which time the majority of the batch returned off lease.

2002 deliveries commenced in March and April, the batch arriving early. Numbered DPS624 to DPS640 (SK02XGT-X, XHD-H/J/L-P/R) they were allocated to Stamford Brook where they were used on the 283 (East Acton-Shepherd's Bush-Hammersmith-Barnes Pond). They continued on the route until February 2011, at which time they moved to Harrow where they replaced the SDP class saloons.

Eight more 8.8m MPDs arrived in May 2002, this time at Stamford Brook. Numbered DPK616-623 (LG02FEX, FFA-E/H/J) they were used on the 272 (Chiswick-Shepherd's Bush Green). In March 2005, DPK616/7 transferred to Tolworth for use on the K5 when the route was taken over at short notice. They remained there until August 2006 when two new MPDs were delivered. In May 2007, the 272 was lost with some moving to Tolworth, another three moving to Harrow.

Between June and August, DPS641 to DPS680 were delivered to London United. Registration marks LG02FFK-P/R-Z, FGA/C-F/J/K/M-P/U/V/X/Z, FHA-F/H/J/K/L were allocated to the batch. Tolworth took delivery of DPS641-60 for use on the 265 between Putney Bridge Station and Tolworth. They were shared with the 418 (Kingston-Epsom), displacing MCW Metrobuses. DPS661-672 arrived in July for route 391 (Richmond-Sands End), these being allocated to Stamford Brook. DPS661-3 were loaned in November 2005 to Metroline, operating from North Wembley. At the same time, DPS664 to DPS667 were loaned to Stagecoach London at Bromley for use on the Bromley Park & Ride. DPS673-680 were the final members of this batch to arrive in August. They were ordered for route 419, but the route was not ready for low-floor operation at this time, and the batch went into store. By November, DPS675-80 had entered service on the 419, operating the route from Hounslow. DPS673 and DPS674

The closing months of 2001 saw the arrival of the intended batch of DPS class Dart SLFs for the 285. DPS575 (SN51SZL) was one of this batch and is seen arriving at Kingston's Cromwell Road bus station. Route branding was applied to this batch of vehicles as can be seen. *Ian Armstrong Collection*

The introduction of the 8.8m long variant of Pointer Dart SLF saw a third classification code for the combination, this being DPK. The first batch arrived for routes K2 and K3 but were also found operating other Kingston area services from time to time. This was the case when the camera captured DPK615 (SN51SXJ) in Kingston, operating local service K4. *Liam Farrer-Beddall*

found homes at Stamford Brook. Despite entering service at the end of the year, this batch retained their 02-registration marks. DPS668-680 were transferred to Fulwell along with 391 in November 2005, returning to Stamford Brook in May 2007 along with the 391. In November, some of the batch were transferred to Shepherd's Bush for use on the 72. In October 2008 they were put to use on the K50 park & ride service in Kingston, operating from Tolworth.

The final new batch of DPS class Dart SLFs arrived in May 2003. Hounslow took delivery of DPS681-5 (SN03LDY/Z, LEF/J/U) from where they were used on route 110 (Twickenham-Hounslow). DPS686-694 (SN03LFA/B/D/E-H/J/K) followed, with all but one being allocated to Hounslow Heath for use on the 216 (Kingston-Staines). The final member of the batch, DPS694, was allocated to Stamford Brook.

The original batch of low-floor Dart SLFs, DP1-11, was taken off the 81 in the autumn of 2005, being replaced by dual-doored buses. After this they were used on the K50 Kingston Park & Ride service. Once the seasonal service had finished, they were made redundant and were placed with various garages around the company, putting in regular appearances on the 467. Stamford Brook took delivery of the batch in early 2006 for use on route 440, displacing the CD class Dart SLFs. DP2-7 were later loaned to various London United garages to allow the fleet to get ibus equipment. DP8/9 were allocated to Hounslow for use on school routes 697 and 698.

It was mentioned above that London United took on route K5 at short notice in March 2005 seeing a pair of DPK class Dart SLFs transfer to Tolworth to take up the route. They were replaced in August 2006 by two new 8.8m MPDS, DPK624/5 (SN06JPV/X). Upon arrival, these vehicles duly took up service on the K5 between Ham and Morden Station.

Four Alexander ALX200 bodied Transbus Dart saloons were hired from the East London Bus Group in October 2006. Allocated to Hounslow, they were used to cover for native Darts whilst they underwent refurbishment. The vehicles concerned were numbered 34272 to 34275 (Y272-4, 354FJN), returning the same month.

A number of DPS class Dart SLFs were transferred to London Sovereign at Harrow in 2008. DPS513 was first to make the move in January. No more followed until

DPS647 (LG02FFR) represents the forty-strong batch of DPS class Dart SLFs to arrive over the summer of 2002. It is seen at the Putney Bridge Station terminus of route 265. *Ian Armstrong Collection*

Eight 8.8m long Pointer MPDs arrived at Stamford Brook for route 272 in June 2002. By May 2007 the type had left Stamford Brook, with the last three transferring to the Sovereign operation at Harrow. DPK622 (LG02FFN) was one of the vehicles to make this move. It is seen on layover at Harrow bus station whilst operating route H10. *David Beddall*

September when DPS571-9 transferred following the introduction of Enviro 200s on the 285. DPS559-70 followed in October.

DPS598 (SN51TEO) was given an all-over advertisement for Roehampton University in November 2008.

Twenty-seven 10.1m ADL Pointer Darts were taken into stock by London United in November 2009 when the company acquired the business and vehicles of NCP Challenger of Twickenham. They took up stock numbers DPS701-727 (SN55HKD/E-H/J-M/O/P/T/U/V-Y, HSD/E HKZ, HLA/C, DVR/T-W). Operating from a base in Twickenham, this batch was used on routes 33 and 419. The Darts on the 33 were replaced by Enviro 200s in 2010, the DPSs being transferred within London United for further service. DPS701-6 were retained by Twickenham for use on the 419.

Thirty Plaxton Pointer bodied Dennis Dart SLFs were transferred to London Sovereign in 2009, replacing the SDP class Dart SLFs which returned off loan. DPS624 was the first, being transferred in March. It was followed by DPS583 in April. DPS559 and 625 moved to Harrow in June, whilst DPS579, 587/9-92/5/6 transferred in July. October 2009 saw the transfer of DPS511/2/4/6-9, 523/6, 544/6/7. These were followed in November by DPS521/2/4. The final movement for 2009 took place in December, when DPS626, 630 and 634 all moved to Harrow. Some of this was achieved by the double-decking of route 81 in October 2009, releasing ten DFs for use at Hounslow Heath.

A further twenty-one Pointer Darts were transferred during 2010. In January, DPS528, 629/32/3/5-9 made the move to Harrow, followed in February by DPS627.

East London Bus Group's 34275 (Y354FJN) was the last of four Alexander ALX200 bodied Dennis Dart SLF saloons to be hired by London United in October 2006. They were allocated to Hounslow and primarily used on the 81 between Hounslow and Slough. 34275 is seen parked at Hounslow bus station. *David Beddall*

Twenty-seven additional ADL Pointer Darts were acquired in November 2009 from NSL Services (originally NCP Challenger). They were reallocated within the London United operation. DPS711 (SN55HKP) is seen on layover at Hounslow bus station before heading back to Ashford Hospital on the 116. *Liam Farrer-Beddall*

DPS527, 531 and 533 were transferred to Harrow in April. In August, DPS628 and DPS640 moved to Harrow. They were joined by DPS532 and 536 in September. DPS534, 543 and 548 were transferred to Harrow in October. The final vehicle transferred in December, when DPS581 moved to Harrow.

The operations of Transdev London were divided into two in February 2011. London Sovereign took Harrow and Edgware garages, with RATP taking over the London United and NCP operations. The DPS class Pointer Dart SLFs listed above transferred to London Sovereign. Later in 2011, a number of the Dart SLFs were replaced by Enviro 200s.

The RATP London fleet was renumbered into a five-digit numbering scheme in March 2016. At this time, DP1/7, 10/1 were renumbered 30401/7/10/1, whilst DPS590-727 were renumbered 30590-727 (with gaps).

By the end of 2018, the once large batch of Dart SLFs was down to a handful, operating on route 72 at Shepherd's Bush. DPS30687 was the last of the type to operate on the route, being withdrawn on 23 June 2019. DP30671/3 were used almost up to this date.

Route 72 was the last route to see regular Dart operation in 2019. DPS30687 (SN03LFB) was the last Dart to be operated in passenger service by London United and is seen shortly before withdrawal in June 2019. The Westfield shopping centre at White City can be seen in the background. *Liam Farrer-Beddall*

KENTISH BUS/ARRIVA KENT THAMESIDE

Kentish Bus was the new name for the former London Country South East operations, being renamed as such in 1987.

The first Dennis Darts entered the Kentish Bus fleet in October 1993 when the operations and vehicles of Transcity of Sidcup were acquired. At this time, nine 9.0m Plaxton Pointer bodied Darts were taken into stock, being used on the 286 between Eltham and Greenwich. The green-based livery of their previous owner was soon replaced by the Kentish Bus maroon and pale primrose livery. The vehicles concerned were registered J220/1/3-9HGY, numbered 100/1, 103-9 by Kentish Bus. 103 to 109 passed to Metrobus in January 1996, whilst 100 and 101 remained in use until August 1997, after which time they passed to Maidstone & District.

The company, however, may be better known for operating the largest batch of Northern Counties Paladin bodied Darts in the London area. Forty-eight of the type were purchased during 1994 after a number of LRT contract gains in south-east

101 (J221HGY) was one of nine Plaxton Pointer bodied Dennis Dart saloons acquired by Kentish Bus from Transcity of Sidcup. It is seen out of service, parked in Eltham wearing full Kentish Bus livery. *Ian Armstrong Collection*

London. They also crossed the River Thames on routes 42 and 108. Other routes they acquired were the 126 and 162 in the Bromley area, along with the 225 and 286. The maroon and pale primrose livery was again applied to these vehicles, making them stand out from the traditional red buses. To accommodate these vehicles, two garages were established in the London area, one in Lewisham, the initial base for the fleet, before a second opened at the former London Buses Ash Grove garage, this latter site being known as Cambridge Heath by Kentish Bus. This latter location was the home garage of the 42. The fleet of Darts were numbered 112-29, 131-46 and 148-157 by Kentish Bus, and carried registration marks L112-29/31-46/8-57YVK. Despite their initial success, Kentish Bus only retained these routes for a short period, losing all but the 126 on re-tender. The displaced Darts went on to replace midibuses in the main Kentish Bus fleet in Kent, with the Darts allocated to Lewisham transferring to either Dartford or Dunton Green.

Kentish Bus was renamed Arriva Kent Thameside in November 1997, the maroon and primrose livery giving way to the standard Arriva turquoise and cream livery.

The closure of Cambridge Heath in February 1998 meant that the Paladins transferred to Arriva London North East, being used on the 225. As mentioned under the Arriva London heading, some of the batch later moved to Arriva London North at Ponders End for use on the 192. By this time, those used on the 126 had lost the original Kentish Bus livery in favour of Arriva's corporate livery. The Paladins were replaced on the 126 by new Pointer bodied Dart SLFs in March 2001.

The former London Country South West and South East operations were eventually amalgamated under the Arriva Southern Counties operation, after numerous different names were used during the 1990s. A large fleet of Dennis Dart SLFs were purchased by the company and could be found across the operating area from Guildford in Surrey

Liverpool Street finds Kentish Bus Northern Counties bodied Dart 125 (L125YVK) wearing full Kentish Bus livery. The 42 was one of two routes to operate into north London. *David Moth*

The rolling stock on the 286 was renewed in February 1998, the step entrance Pointer Darts being replaced by new low-floor Pointer bodied Dart SLFs, which wore full Arriva corporate livery as seen above. 3265 (R265EKO) represents the batch. Note the small roundel on the nearside. *Ian Armstrong Collection*

to Maidstone in Kent. A few of these batches were used on London contracts, along with some operating into the Greater London region. Those operated by the former London & Country operation can be found listed under that heading.

Twelve 10.7m long Pointer Dart SLFs were purchased by Arriva Kent Thameside, arriving in February 1998. Numbered 3261 to 3272 (R261-72EKO) they were used on the 286 (Greenwich-Queen Mary Hospital). They originally wore the turquoise and cream Arriva livery. 3266 was the first to get the red livery, this being done in November 2003, and was used on the 428. Other members of the batch joined 3266 during 2006. New rolling stock replaced the fleet on the 286 in July 2007. By this time 3262/4/5/6/9/70/1 had received the red London livery and were transferred to Grays for further use on the 370 (Grays-Romford). The others were reallocated around the Arriva Southern Counties fleet for further use. In April 2008, those at Grays found a new home with Arriva Kent & Sussex at Tunbridge Wells, where they replaced older vehicles on the 402 between Tunbridge Wells and Bromley, lasting on the route until 2011 when Optare Versas replaced them on the route.

The next batch of fourteen 10.7m Pointer Darts arrived in March 1999 numbered 3276 to 3289 (T276-89JKM). They were used to extend a number of routes from Dartford to Bluewater. The first thirteen members of the batch were split between routes 428 (Erith-Dartford-Bluewater) and 477 (Orpington-Dartford-Bluewater). The last member of the batch was allocated to Northfleet. Those used on the 428 were painted red in 2003 and 2004, being used until early 2009 when new Enviro 200s took over. After this time, they were reallocated to Arriva Southend. Those on the 477 retained standard Arriva livery, as the 477 was not a TfL service.

A couple of years passed before the next batch of Pointer Dart SLFs arrived for use on TfL contracts. The vehicles in question were numbered 3291-9 and 3301-3 (Y291-9, 301-3TKJ), arriving in March 2001 for route 126 (Eltham-Bromley South), replacing Northern Counties bodied Darts. These also wore the standard Arriva turquoise and cream livery and measured 10.6m. The original livery was lost when they were repainted red.

The final batch of Dart SLFs for Arriva Kent Thameside arrived in April 2006. 1624 to 1632 (SN06BPE/F/KU/V/X/Y/Z) were shorter 8.8m long Plaxton Pointer MPD bodied Dennis Dart SLF saloons. They were purchased for use on the 162 between Beckenham Junction and Eltham Station, taken over from Stagecoach in February 2006. They were late arriving, and Arriva hired nine MPDs from Stagecoach London, these being 34212-4/7/8, 34220-3. 1624 to 1632 were delivered in the Arriva London red livery. The Company lost the 162 upon retender to Metrobus in March 2011. After this they were initially used where needed within the Arriva Southern Counties Group, before transferring to Arriva London North at Enfield and Lea Valley garages, taking up stock numbers PDL137 to PDL145 with their new owner.

Chislehurst finds
1624 (SN06BPE), the newest Dart to be purchased by Arriva Kent Thameside. It is seen on its way to Beckenham Junction.
Collin Lloyd/Jeff Lloyd

LONDON & COUNTRY

Route H28 was London & Country's first London route operated by the Dennis Dart. Four East Lancs EL2000 bodied Darts initially operated the route. 522 (M522MPF) is seen in Hounslow heading towards Bull's. Bridge. *Collin Lloyd/Jeff Lloyd Collection*

London & Country operated a large number of Darts and Dart SLF saloons in the former London Country South West area, serving Sussex and Surrey.

The Company purchased ten East Lancs EL2000 bodied Dennis Darts in 1995 which they allocated to Leatherhead. Four of the batch were put to use on the H28 (Osterley-Hounslow Garage). This was a new midibus route introduced in February 1995, supported by the London Borough of Hounslow. In December 1995 it was extended to operate between Osterley Tesco and Bull's Bridge. The vehicles were taken into stock in May, carrying stock numbers 521 to 524 (M521-4HPF). Although officially allocated to Leatherhead, these vehicles operated from an outstation set up in Albion Road, Hounslow. A month later, in June, they were joined by two additional vehicles of the same type. They carried on the numbering sequence as 525 and 526 (M525/6MPM). They were put to use on the 441 linking Englefield Green, Egham and Staines with Heathrow Airport. In January 1996 520 to 526 got new rolling stock numbers DS10 to DS15 respectively. The route transferred to Tellings-Golden Miller in July 1999, the vehicles going on loan for a short time.

London & Country took delivery of their first low-floor Dennis Dart SLFs in May 1996 when twelve 10.0m 35-seaters were purchased for the take up of London route 105 (Heathrow Airport-Greenford Station). The route had originally been taken over using step-entrance Darts. A new base was set up on the Kelvin Industrial Estate in Greenford in order to operate the service. The two-tone green and red livery was applied to the batch of vehicles, with route branding being applied in October. Registration marks N225-36TPK were allocated to the vehicles, which took up fleet numbers DSL25 to DSL36.

Nineteen 9.4m long East Lancs Spryte bodied Dart SLFs were taken into stock by London & Country in July 1996. Three of this batch, DSL38 (N238VPH) and DSL50/1 (P250/1APM), supported the Pointer Darts on the 105. However, operational difficulties were experienced on the route, and by November it transferred to Centrewest who operated it from Alperton. The fleet of Dart SLFs went on loan to Centrewest until February 1998 when they returned to London & Country.

A further forty-one Pointer Darts were taken into stock by London & Country during 1997, seven of which were allocated to Leatherhead. DSL90 to DSL96 (P290-6FPK) were used on route 465 between Kingston and Dorking. Leatherhead was closed in May 1999, at which time the route passed to Tellings-Golden Miller along with the vehicles. Retaining the green and red livery, Tellings-Golden Miller numbered the vehicles 590 to 596 and used them until July 2002 when they were returned to Arriva, being allocated to Guildford.

A fleet of Enviro 200 single-decks was added to the 465 in 2007. However, the route was in need of a spare to cover maintenance. At this time a solitary Pointer Dart SLF numbered 3179 (P179LKL) was allocated to Horsham for use on the route. 3179 was a much-travelled Dart SLF, seeing service with Arriva Southern Counties at Maidstone, Dartford and Grays. The Horsham operation was sold to Metrobus in October 2009, with 3179 passing initially to the new owner but was soon sold.

N236TPK is the last of eleven Pointer Dart SLFs purchased by London & Country for route 105. It is seen bound for Heathrow Airport whilst passing through Greenford. *Colin Lloyd/Jeff Lloyd*

LONDONLINKS

Sutton finds
Londonlinks Plaxton Pointer bodied Dennis Dart M162SKR. These vehicles looked smart in the two-tone green and red stripe livery of Londonlinks. *Ian Armstrong Collection*

Londonlinks purchased four new Pointer bodied Darts in 1995, arriving in May. 160 to 163 (M160-3SKR) were allocated to Croydon from where they operated the 407. They wore a two-tone green livery when new.

Kentish Bus lost the 42 and the 108 in April 1997. After this time, eight of the large fleet of Northern Counties Paladin bodied Dennis Dart saloons transferred across to Londonlinks at Croydon, displacing MetroRiders on the 407. The vehicles concerned were numbered DS120-6 and DS151 (L120-6/51YVK).

A re-organisation of Arriva's operations in October 1999 meant that these two batches of Darts transferred to the control of Arriva London South, initially being allocated to Beddington Farm. They saw further service with Arriva London, details of which can be found under the operators heading.

Northern Counties Paladin bodied Dennis Dart DS122 (L122YVK) was new to sister company Kentish Bus. It is also seen working route 407 and is again photographed in Sutton. *Ian Armstrong Collection*

DOCKLANDS MINIBUS

The name Docklands Minibus has already been mentioned in this book under the Stagecoach London section. The company was originally owned by Transit Holdings Limited and operated a number of minibuses around the Docklands area of London on a number of non-LRT services, as well as operating Mercedes-Benz minibuses on routes 287, 366 and 368. The Company was successful in winning the contract for the 106 (Finsbury Park-Whitechapel) which commenced in April 1996. For this, eighteen Plaxton Pointer bodied Dennis Dart saloons were ordered. Prior to their arrival, a similar dual-doored vehicle was taken on loan from fellow Transit Holdings operation Thames Transit of Oxford. M58VJO was the vehicle in question and operated in London during February 1996. The intended batch duly arrived during April registered N410-27MBW.

A second batch of Pointer Darts was also ordered by the company, meant as a replacement for the original batch of Darts on the 106. The N-MBW batch was then going to be used to displace the older Mercedes-Benz minibuses operating the routes mentioned above. However, before this new order materialised, on 22 July 1997 the Stagecoach Group acquired the business of Transit Holdings Ltd. As has already been mentioned, Docklands Minibus was therefore placed under the control of Stagecoach East London. The new company took on the order of these Pointer bodied Darts, with details of this batch being found under the Stagecoach London heading.

Eighteen Pointer Darts were purchased by Docklands Transit to operate route 106. 412 (N412MBW) is seen at Finsbury Park Station before starting its journey to Whitechapel wearing the smart red, white and blue livery. *Ian Armstrong Collection*

ARMCHAIR

The first Dennis Darts entered the Armchair, Brentford fleet in August 1996 when the company took over operation of route 117 (Staines-Isleworth Fire Station) from London & Country. Seven Plaxton Pointer bodied Darts registered P27-9, 31/2/4/5MLE were taken into stock during July for use on this service. December saw the arrival of six similar vehicles, with a slightly higher seating capacity. P154/6-60MLE were put to use on the 190 during this month. All wore the distinctive orange livery with white and black bands.

There were further tender wins in the Ealing area in the spring of 1997, with routes E2 (Greenford-Ealing Broadway-Brentford) and E8 (Ealing Broadway Station-Brentford) being won. Twenty-five single-doored 10.0m long Plaxton Pointer bodied Dennis Dart SLFs were ordered, arriving with the company during April and May. Allocated registration marks P675-99RWU, this batch remained true to the two services until they were replaced by new rolling stock in 2002. The new style registrations introduced in September 2001 led to this batch being numbered DP675-99. P693RWU hung on with the company after the others had departed, being used on various contracts, before transferring to Metroline in November 2003.

Armchair took delivery of its first Dennis Darts during 1996 when, in August, seven Plaxton Pointer bodied saloons were purchased for route 117. P28MLE was one of this batch, and as route 190 gained a batch of similar vehicles, they could could be found operating either service. It is seen in Richmond shortly before reaching the end of the 190 at the bus station. *Ian Armstrong Collection*

Thirteen Alexander ALX200 bodied Dart SLFs were purchased for route 209 (Hammersmith-Mortlake). Strengthening work on Hammersmith Bridge during 1999 meant that these vehicles were swapped onto London United's route 49, the latter operator continuing to operate the 209 until the weight limit was lifted. The ALX200s arrived in May 1999 registered T140-152AUA, gaining fleet numbers DA140 to DA152 in February 2002.

The batch of ALX200s did not match the total number of vehicles required for the PVR on the 49. Therefore, Armchair hired three Plaxton Pointer MPDs to make up numbers.

Operating in dealer white, they were registered T546/8/9HNH. Armchair finally took over route 209 in October 1999, after which time two of the MPDs were retained for use on the K50 Kingston Park & Ride service. Five 10.7m long Pointer Dart SLFs also arrived with Armchair for this service, the MPDs proving to be too small. After the contract had finished, T549HNH was retained by Armchair, receiving a repaint into fleet livery, being used on the 117 and 190.

The following year, another five Pointer Dart SLFs were loaned for use on the K50. These vehicles carried registration marks P827BUD, R660GCA, T443EBD, T419MNH and V338SVV. They were supported by East Lancs Spryte bodied Dart SLF W682TNV. They were loaned between November 2000 and January 2001. Another Plaxton Pointer bodied Dennis Dart SLF was also loaned from Dawson Rentals between April and July, being used on the 485 for the duration of its stay.

T549HNH was replaced on the 485 in July 2001 by a new Pointer MPD Y962KRX. The numbering of the fleet in February 2002 meant that this saloon was given stock number DP962.

The two original batches of Pointer Darts were replaced between September 2001 and January 2002. First to go were those operating the 117. Eight Pointer Dart SLFs

Armchair received its first low-floor Darts in early 1997 for routes E2 and E8. The penultimate member of the batch, P698RWU, is seen operating route E2 showing off the smart white, orange and black Armchair livery. *Ian Armstrong Collection*

The second batch of low-floor Dart SLFs arrived in May 1999 for route 209. This time the Alexander ALX200 body style was selected. DA143 (T143AUA) is seen at a sunny Hammersmith bus station. *David Beddall*

Y962KRX was purchased by Armchair as a more permanent vehicle on route 485. It replaced a hired vehicle registered T549HNH. It is seen parked at Richmond bus station in full Armchair livery. *Ian Armstrong Collection*

registered Y63LTF, RX51FNP/S/T/U/V/W/Y. They soon took up stock numbers DP1004, 1000-3, 1007/6/5/8. At this time the 117 was extended beyond Isleworth, to the West Middlesex Hospital. The second batch was used on the 190, being allotted registration marks RL51DNU/V/X/Y, DOA/H/J/U. A month after arrival they were numbered DP1016/4/0/3, 1009, 1012/1/5. These were the first vehicles to wear the new orange, red and black livery.

The final large batch of Plaxton Pointer bodied Dennis Dart SLFs was delivered between May and August 2002, replacing the P-RWU batch of single-doored Dart SLFs on the E2 and E8. They took up rolling stock numbers DP1017 to DP1048 and carried registration marks KP02PUF/H/J/O, PVD/E, PUK, PVF/K/J/L/O/N/T/U, PWN, KU02YUB-D, KP02PWU/V/O, KU02YUE/J/K, KM02HFK/N/L/O, HGD/E/F. With the exception of P693RWU, the rest of the batch returned to Dawson Rentals after the arrival of this new batch. However, in November, P675RWU returned to Armchair and was placed into reserve and P690-2/4-9RWU also returned to Armchair, this time on loan for the seasonal route K50. They returned to Dawson Rentals in February 2003.

T549HNH made a second appearance with Armchair in November 2003, being put to use on the K50. It returned to Dawson Rentals in January 2004. It was joined by eight other Pointer Dart SLFs, these being registered T418MNH, T459/64HNH, T548EBD, W378SVV, W559/68JVV and KX51UCR, these also returning in January 2004. V549JBH came on loan from Mitcham Belle in March 2004, and was used on the 209 and E2 respectively, returning to its rightful owner in September. In May, Go-Ahead London loaned LDP35 (P735RYL) for use on the E2 and E8 until October. These latter two vehicles were loaned as paint floats whilst Armchair repainted its fleet of Dart SLFs.

An increase on the 209 saw the need for an additional vehicle and DP1049 (KX54NJO) arrived in September 2004.

Two months later, Metroline took over the operations, vehicles and garage of Armchair. This initially had no impact on the fleet, apart from the gradual repaint into Metroline livery. Further details of the former Armchair fleet are noted under the Metroline heading.

September 2001 saw the rolling stock on the 117 upgraded to low-floor Dart SLFs. Originally un-numbered, the batch soon received fleet numbers. RX51FNW became DP1005, and is seen parked at Staines bus station. *Ian Armstrong Collection*

CAPITAL CITYBUS

First Group acquired the business of Capital Citybus on 8 July 1998, after which date a large number of low-floor Dart SLF saloons were taken into stock, these being covered under the First London heading earlier in this book. However, before this, Capital Citybus had operated a handful of Dart saloons.

The first Dennis Dart was purchased in July 1994. Registered L670SMC, this vehicle was numbered 670 by the company. It carried a Northern Counties Paladin body and was used on the 246. It initially wore the distinctive yellow livery associated with the Company. It moved on to First Capital in 1998, remaining in London service until January 2002 when it was transferred within First Group.

It wasn't until February 1996 that the next Dart entered the fleet. At this time, J458JOW arrived, carrying the more unusual Wadham Stringer Portsdown bodywork, being one of only two used in the London area. It took up rolling stock number 669, again being withdrawn from London service in January 2002.

Other than a demonstration vehicle loaned to London Buses Limited, Capital Citybus operated the only Wadham Stringer Portsdown bodied Dennis Dart on a London service. Registered J459JOW, it took fleet number 669. It is seen departing Finsbury Park on route 236. *Matthew Wharmby*

The only other Darts to operate with Capital Citybus before the First takeover came in the form of thirteen East Lancs Spryte bodied Dart SLFs. 705 to 718 (R705-18VLA) were allocated to Hackney Wick for use on the S2 (Stratford-Clapton), taken over from Stagecoach London. 705 to 707 arrived in January 1998, the others following in February. The traditional yellow livery, with red band, was applied to these vehicles.

Thirteen East Lancs Spryte bodied Dennis Dart SLF saloons were taken into stock in 1998 by Capital Citybus just prior to First Group purchasing the company. Stratford bus station finds 706 (R706VLA) heading towards Clapton on route S2. *Jeff Lloyd Collection*

LIMEBOURNE

Limebourne Travel was what remained after Q-Drive sold London Buslines and the Berks Bucks Bus Company to Centrewest. Operating from a base on Silverthorne Road, Battersea, the company entered the London bus market in May 1996 after winning the C3.

April 1997 was a good time for the company, as it won its second service, the 42 between Liverpool Street Station and Denmark Hill. Eight 10.0m long Pointer Dart SLFs were hired for use on the route. Registered P301-8HDP, these vehicles wore a red-based livery, with a stone-coloured skirt and a white line, making the company compliant with the 80 per cent red rule introduced by Transport for London. Rolling stock numbers 2301 to 2308 were allotted to these vehicles. Nine additional Pointer Dart SLFs arrived in September for use on the 156 (Clapham Junction-Wimbledon). R309-15/7/9NGM were given fleet numbers 2309-15/7/9. Route branding was applied to this batch of vehicles.

Q-Drive ran into financial difficulty in October 1998, leading to the fleet of Pointer Darts mentioned above being repossessed by the leasing company. Limebourne was soon purchased by the local management, but they had no vehicles to operate the

A batch of Plaxton Pointer bodied Dennis Dart SLFs was purchased by Limebourne in September 1997. They were employed on route 156 and again carried route branding for the service as seen applied to 2310 (R310NGM). It is seen loading near to Clapham Junction on its way to Wimbledon. *Ian Armstrong Collection*

services. The new owners called themselves Independent Way. At this time the new Company could not afford new buses. Help was provided by Armchair, London General, Arriva London, Metrobus, Metroline and Nostalgiabus, who continued to operate the London services until Limebourne could re-establish itself.

A number of second-hand vehicles were sourced by Limebourne, including a number of Volvo single-deckers and Marshall Minibuses. Eleven Carlyle Dartline bodied Darts were acquired to help fill the gaps; these being purchased from Metroline. The vehicles concerned were numbered DT89, 93, 124-6, 134/6, 141/2 and 156/7. They were repainted red with a green skirt prior to them entering service with Limebourne.

Eight Plaxton Pointer bodied Dennis Darts were taken into stock for route G1 in August 1999, which had been sub-contracted from South London. The vehicles concerned were DR20 to DR27 (H120THE, H621TKU, H122-7THE). These worked alongside Carlyle Dartline bodied DT62, 68 and 70 which were loaned from Arriva London, these latter vehicles returning to Arriva in April 2000. The Pointers remained with the Company until it was purchased by Connex in July 2001.

The first new rolling stock entered the fleet in the spring of 1999 after route 344 (Clapham Junction-Elephant & Castle) was won. By this time, Limebourne had ordered new rolling stock for routes 42 and 156, with further new vehicles being ordered after this tender win. Seventeen Caetano Compass bodied Dennis Dart SLFs entered the fleet between March and May 1999, the shortfall of new vehicles being covered by hired double-decks until September when a second batch of Caetano Compass bodied Dart SLFs arrived. The first batch was registered T401-4/6-11/3-9LGP, whilst the September deliveries took registration marks V421-37KGF.

DT157 (H157NON) was the last of eleven Carlyle bodied Darts acquired by Limebourne in 1998. It is seen after a repaint into Limebourne colours. *Collin Lloyd/Jeff Lloyd Collection*

The tender win of route 344 saw additional Caetano Compass bodied Dennis Dart SLFs purchased by Limebourne. The last of the batch, (V437KGF) is seen blinded for the route. *Ian Armstrong Collection*

These dual-doored single-deckers wore a similar livery to the original Limebourne fleet but featured a darker green skirt. T415LGP was an exception to this, having a blue skirt, and was used on the Westminster & Chelsea Hospital shuttle, given route number H1. They were also named after castles.

Connex Bus acquired the business of Limebourne in July 2001, leading to the transfer of the Dart SLFs to the new owner. Those that continued to operate in the London area will be mentioned under the relevant operator.

TELLINGS-GOLDEN MILLER

West London operator Tellings-Golden Miller successfully established itself as a London operator between 1998 and 2005, with a large number of Dennis Darts being operated. The first route to receive Dart SLFs commenced operation in January 1998. R501-14SJM were put to use on the 235 between Brentford and Sunbury. A white-based livery, complete with yellow and blue relief, was worn by this batch.

This was followed by the addition of the Kingston University contract in September 1998. Three additional Pointer Dart SLFs, 515-7 S515-7TCF, were used on this service. S518/9TCF were added to the fleet in December 1998. These were used on Surrey County Council route 471 (Kingston-Dittons-Esher-Hersham-Weybridge-Addlestone-New Haw-West Byfleet-Sheerwater-Woking).

April 1999 saw the transfer of route 465 from London & Country to Tellings-Golden Miller. Seven Pointer Darts transferred between the two operating companies at the same time, retaining their former London & Country identities. DSL90 to DSL96 (P290-6FPK) also retained their green livery worn since new.

The Tellings-Golden Miller fleet stood out from other London operators, using a livery of white, yellow and blue. It wasn't until 1998 that the company took delivery of its first Dennis Dart SLFs. Fourteen were used on route 235, with R505SJM being one of these vehicles. It is seen loading in Hounslow. *Ian Armstrong Collection*

V301-9MDP arrived in November 1999 for the take up of another service, the H20 (Hounslow-Ivybridge), taken over from London United. These were the first 8.8m long Pointer MPDs. They could also be found operating route H26 between Feltham and Hatton Cross. Minibuses were displaced from this latter service by the new rolling stock. The H20 originally operated from the former London & Country garage at Hounslow, whilst the H26 ran out of Capital Logitistics' former West Drayton premises. However, both routes were joined together when operations moved to Fulwell in April 2000.

A trio of white Dart SLFs were hired by Tellings-Golden Miller in February 2000 to allow the company's own fleet to be fitted with wheelchair ramps. The vehicles were registered T553HNH, T445/6EBD. They returned off lease in April.

Routes R68 (Hampton Court Station-Richmond) and R70 (Richmond-Nurseylands) were won from London United in 2000, for which two batches of Pointer bodied Dart SLFs were purchased. Those ordered for the R68 measured 10.1m and were registered W401-4, 407-9, 411-3UGM. The R70 batch measured 10.7m, and was allotted registration marks W601-9, 611/2UGM. A delay in the start of the R70 meant that some of the batch were loaned to Green Triangle, Lancashire, others being stored at Plaxton in Scarborough.

Eight additional Plaxton Pointer MPD bodied Dennis Dart SLF saloons were taken into stock by Tellings-Golden Miller during December 2000 for use on the H28 between Hayes Tesco and Osterley Tesco, via Hounslow. Entering service in January 2001, they replaced step-entrance Darts M521-4HPF and N528-30SPA which had been on loan from London & Country. The vehicles were registered X311-5/7/9/22KRX.

N305DHE was the first Dennis Dart SLF to be taken into stock in 2001, arriving in June from Country Lion, Northampton. Measuring 10.6m, it was allocated to Byfleet for use on contracts in Surrey.

The first Pointer MPDs for the company arrived in November 1999 for use on the H20 and H26. V306MDP is seen loading at Hatton Cross ready for its outbound journey to Feltham. *Ian Armstrong Collection*

A month later a pair of Caetano Compass bodied Dennis Dart SLFs were taken into stock, again being allocated to Byfleet. They were predominantly operated on service 48 between Woking and Farnborough, outside of the traditional London Country operating area. Y40 and 50TGM remained for a year before being sold to Countryliner.

August 2001 saw the arrival of a solitary MPD registered 1068MW and given fleet number 323. It was purchased to operate the R62 between West Middlesex Hospital and Hampton and was allocated to Fulwell. It was the only vehicle to feature blinds for the R62.

Route 203 (Hounslow-Staines) was won by the company at the expense of London Buslines. RX51FGG/K/J/M/N/O/P were taken into stock during August 2001, numbered 414 to 420. These were further 10.1m Pointer Dart SLFs.

Route H25 (Hatton Cross Station-Butts Farm) received new rolling stock in November. Seven 10.2m long Caetano Nimbus bodied Dart SLFs were taken into stock numbered 421 to 427. These vehicles were registered RA51KKF/G/H/D/E, KLE, and KGE. A member of the batch was displayed at the NEC in October 2001, leading to the loan of a demonstrator registered X93FOR.

Plaxton Pointer RA51KVS was the final new vehicle delivered to the company in 2001, arriving in November. Numbered 324, it was put to use on the 513 group of services from Byfleet.

The demise of White Rose Travel in February 2002 meant that Tellings-Golden Miller could take on routes 218 (Kingston-Esher-Shepperton-Laleham-Staines), the 566/567 (Staines to Knowle Hill) and Saturday only service 218 between Staines and Shepperton. To operate these services, a number of Dart SLFs were taken on loan carrying various bodywork. P942EMS carried Alexander ALX200 bodywork, whilst R526YRP carried an East Lancs Spryte body. The other four carried Plaxton Pointer bodies. These were registered S396HVV, V377SVV, X371CUY and KP51SXY.

Tellings-Golden Miller successfully won the contracts for the R68 and R70 routes in the Richmond area from London United. For these, two batches of Pointer bodied Dart SLFs were purchased. W407UGM was one of the R68 batch, route branding was applied to these vehicles. *Ian Armstrong Collection*

A pair of Caetano Compass bodied Dart SLFs arrived to operate non-London route 48 in Surrey. Y50TGM was one of the duo and is seen in Kingston off route operating the 471 to New Haw. Both were allocated to Tellings-Golden Miller's Byfleet garage. *Ian Armstrong Collection*

Fleet renewal on the H25 saw a change of body style. These were the first of a number of Caetano Nimbus bodied Dart SLFs to be purchased by the company. 421 (RA51KKF) is seen completing its journey at Hatton Cross *Ian Armstrong Collection*

V377SVV was one of a number of Dennis Dart SLFs with varying bodywork to be hired in 2002 by Tellings-Golden Miller for routes 566 and 567, taken on when White Rose Travel collapsed. It is seen parked in Staines. *Ian Armstrong Collection*

Twelve 10.1m Transbus Pointers arrived over the summer of 2002. The first six arrived in June and were used on the 465 (Fulwell-Dorking), replacing Dart SLFs owned by Arriva Southern Counties. It was intended that a batch of Caetano Nimbus bodied Dart SLFs were to operate the 465. Members of the batch were numbered 434-9 (KM02HFP/R/S/T/U/V). The loaned Darts were then put to further use on the 490, displacing Optare Excels, which in turn moved on to the 216 (Kingston-Staines). RD02BJK/O/U/V/X/Z, 440-5, were delivered in August and were put to use on the 490. These were the first vehicles in the fleet to receive a red-based livery, with blue skirts, in line with the 80 per cent rule.

X93FOR, the Caetano Nimbus demonstrator, returned on loan to the company in July 2002, remaining on it until September when it returned to Caetano. In November it was acquired by Tellings-Golden Miller, taking stock number 193. It was mostly used on the 235.

A second batch of Caetano Nimbus bodied Darts, measuring 10.5m, was allocated to Fulwell on route 465. Numbered 428 to 433, this batch was registered RL02FOT/U, FVM/N, ZTB/C.

A collection of hired Dart SLFs being used from Byfleet was replaced by thirteen former Armchair Pointer Dart SLFs in September 2002. P677-89RWU took up stock numbers 477-89 and were used on services 451 (Kingston-Staines) and 461 (Kingston-Woking). They retained the livery of their former owner but were given Tellings-Golden Miller fleet names. They remained with the company until January 2003 when they returned off-lease.

The next batch of Pointer MPDs was allocated to Byfleet garage between December 2002 and January 2003. 325 to 335 (KN52NFO/R/T/U/V/X/Y, NFC/D/E) were used to replace the former Armchair Dart SLFs. Used on routes 218, 451, 461, 566 and 567, they wore the traditional white, blue and yellow livery.

2002 saw the livery change to 80 per cent red, relieved by a blue skirt and yellow line. 438 (KM02HFU) is seen operating route 465 to Fulwell. These were ordered for routes 490 and 216. *Ian Armstrong Collection*

After a couple of loans to Tellings-Golden Miller, demonstrator X93FOR was acquired by the company in November 2002. It received fleet number 193 and is seen stopped in Brentford. *Ian Armstrong Collection*

December 2002 also saw the arrival of a solitary second-hand MPD registered Y38YVV. This vehicle had operated with a number of operators in Surrey and Kent. Acquired from Countryliner, it was numbered 338, and was allocated to Fulwell for route H26.

The arrival of a third batch of Caetano Nimbus bodied Darts took place in the opening months of 2003, these being used to upgrade the rolling stock on the 235. Numbered 613 to 633, these vehicles were registered RN52EOE/D/C/B/V/W/X, ERO/V/U, EYK/L, FRF, FPC/A, FRD, FVR/S, FXD. 613 to 620 arrived in January, the rest arriving in February. This batch replaced the original batch of Dart SLFs. 501-5 were retained by the company, repainted silver for use on service 441 (Heathrow-Staines-Englefield Green). Route branding was also added to these vehicles. 506-10 were also retained, being used from Byfleet.

Ten 8.8m MPDs were delivered to Fulwell in June 2003, these arriving in a silver livery for other services centred on Heathrow Airport, supported by the British Airport Authority (BAA). These were for use on routes 555/6/7, won from London United. This batch of Darts took up fleet numbers 339 to 348 and were registered KV03ZFM/N/P/R/S/T/U/V/W/X/Y.

A month later, a solitary Caetano Nimbus bodied Dart, RN03KEU, was acquired. The chassis was constructed in 1998 and remained unregistered until 2003. Just before being acquired, it was fitted with a Caetano Nimbus body. It was re-registered GB03TGM in April 2004.

The business of Wings Buses was acquired by Tellings-Golden Miller in March 2004. This brought with it a number of Dart SLFs, with both Plaxton Pointer and East Lancs Spryte bodywork. Those carrying Plaxton Pointer bodies were registered SK02TZN/O/P/R/S/T/U/V/W/X, which took fleet numbers 339 to 348. These were used on the E6 between Bull's Bridge and Greenford. The East Lancs Spryte bodied Dart SLFs were registered in two separate registration series, V336-8MBV and W435-8CRN. Rolling stock numbers 451 to 457 were allocated to them. The first three wore a red, orange and

During the turn of 2002 and 2003 Tellings-Golden Miller took delivery of eleven short 8.8m long Pointer MPD bodied Dart SLFs. They were used on a number of services from Byfleet garage. 328 (KN52NFT) is seen loading at Staines bus station before setting out to Virginia Water on route 566. *Ian Armstrong Collection*

yellow livery and were used on the U7 (Uxbridge Station-Charville Lane Estate), whilst the other four were painted in a two-tone green livery and used on the H50 between West Drayton and Stockley Business Park.

Two further batches of Caetano Nimbus bodied Transbus Darts arrived in 2004, during April. Four arrived at this time numbered 447 to 450 (KX04HRD-G). They were allocated to Dartford and were used on Orpington area route R2. However, these only lasted with the company until 5 March 2005, when the route and vehicles transferred to Metrobus.

The second batch was numbered 458 to 463 (HX04HTP/T/U/V/Y/Z). They arrived in July 2004 and were used on the 112 between Ealing Broadway and Brent Cross. They had arrived numbered 451 to 456 but were renumbered, as the former Wings East Lancs bodied Dart SLFs had taken up these numbers.

The Link Line operation of Tellings-Golden Miller received a pair of Caetano Nimbus bodied Darts in 2004, joining other Dennis Dart SLFs in the fleet. This pair took up stock numbers 65 and 66 and measured 9.0m in length. Registration marks HX04HUH and HX04HUK were carried by these vehicles.

The final pair of Dart SLFs to arrive with Tellings-Golden Miller did so in October 2004. X371CUY and KP51SXY arrived from Eurtons of Haverhill. They were allocated to Fulwell, numbered 320 and 321 they were used on services from Byfleet.

The business and vehicles of Tellings-Golden Miller were acquired by the National Express Group in June 2005. They were added to the Travel London operation, which had been formed in February 2004 after purchasing the business of Connex. The majority of the Dennis Dart SLF fleet mentioned above were taken over by this new owner, further details of which can be found later in this book.

HX04HTZ is seen entering Ealing Broadway, the terminus of route 112. It is seen with Tellings-Golden Miller's successor, Travel London. *Jeff Lloyd Collection*

F.E. THORPE

F.E. Thorpe was no stranger to London tendering work, having operated the Stationlink and a number of mobility routes for some years. Route 210 (Finsbury Park Station-Brent Cross) was won in September 1998. A fleet of twelve Pointer bodied Dart SLFs were taken into stock, numbered DLF29 to DLF40 (S529-40JLM). They were allocated to a new operating base in Wembley, wearing a yellow and red livery. Route branding was applied to the batch. Former Limebourne Travel R309NGM was acquired in January 1999 to provide maintenance cover for the 210. It received fleet number DLF9. In January 2000, it was allocated to the Millennium Dome emergency fleet, soon returning to the 210 after not being used.

P41MLE arrived with the company during April 1999, taking stock number DLF41. It was acquired by F.E. Thorpe as a spare vehicle for the Stationlink services SL1 and SL2. Unlike DLF9, this vehicle was dual-doored.

Route 70 (South Kensington-Acton) was the next route to be taken over by F.E. Thorpe. For this, a batch of fourteen 10.1m Pointer Dart SLFs arrived in June 2000. Numbered DLF63-9, 71-7 (W963TRP etc), this batch wore a revised livery of red and yellow. DLF30/1 were used as spare vehicles for the route. An additional Pointer Dart was required, leading to the acquisition of DLF79 (X179BNH) in January 2001, this acting as a spare for the route.

September 1998 saw the arrival of twelve Plaxton Pointer bodied Dennis Dart SLF saloons with F.E. Thorpe for use on the 210 between Finsbury Park and Brent Cross. The batch wore a smart livery of red and yellow. Route branding was also applied to the fleet. DLF39 (S539JLM) is seen loading for Brent Cross at Archway Station. *Ian Armstrong Collection*

Former Limebourne Travel R309NGM was acquired by F.E. Thorpe in January 1999 to act as a spare for route 210. Numbered DLF9 it is seen in between duties at Brent Cross shopping centre, branded for the 210. *Ian Armstrong Collection*

X179BNH arrived with F.E. Thorpe in January 2001 as an extra vehicle for route 70. It received rolling stock number DLF79. *Collin Lloyd/ Jeff Lloyd Collection*

A third batch of Pointer Darts arrived in 2002, numbered DLF80 to DLF103. This batch of twenty-four was used on the 316 (Neasden-North Kensington). The first two were ordered early for use on the Stationlink service, providing cover for the Optare Excels which were proving to be unreliable. Registrations KM02HDJ and HDK were carried by DLF80 and DLF81; whilst the rest of the batch were registered KU52YLG/H, YKN/O/P/R/S/T/V/X/Y/A-H/J/K. The first two arrived in July, whilst the outstanding vehicles were delivered during October.

August 2002 saw the replacement of the Stationlink services which connected Central London rail termini. F.E. Thorpe lost the northern part of the route, retaining the southern part which was numbered 705. This linked Paddington with Victoria, Waterloo and Liverpool Street. The Optare Excels were originally used on this service until seven new Transbus Pointer Darts were taken into stock in October. These vehicles carried on from the 316 batch, numbered DLF104-110 (KU52YKZ, YLA-F). These vehicles were built to a single-door layout.

These were joined on the 705 by all-white liveried Y641AVV. This was longer than other Pointer Dart SLFs in the fleet, measuring 10.7m. After the arrival of this batch, it moved onto the 487, working alongside Volvo B6BLEs. It left F.E. Thorpe in the summer of 2003, only to be reacquired in July 2004, taking stock number DLF125.

A solitary Marshall Capital bodied Dart SLF arrived with F.E. Thorpe during October 2002. However, it wasn't until September 2003 that it entered service. Measuring 10.2m the vehicle concerned was registered AJ02ZRY. It was built to single-door layout, and was numbered MLF122 by the company, being used on the 210.

Before the arrival of DLF125, ten 9.9m Pointer Dart SLFs were loaned to F.E. Thorpe from Mitcham Belle. DLF111-20 (V540/2-50JBH) were used to replace the Volvo B6BLE saloons inherited from Metropolitan Omnibus, being used on the 210, replacing other Dart SLFs which moved on to routes 187 and 487. The 487 was lost in March 2004, the loan batch going on to other London companies for further service.

August 2002 saw two routes replace the Stationlink route in Central London. F.E. Thorpe won the southern service, the 705, for which seven Pointer Dart SLFs were purchased. DLF106 (KU52YLB) is seen passing Victoria Coach Station bound for Liverpool Street Station. *Ian Armstrong Collection*

The final pair of Pointer Darts arrived in November 2003. These 10.1m dual-doored saloons were numbered DLF124 and DLF125, registered KX53SDU/V. However, in August 2004, DLF125 was renumbered to DLF123.

In the same month, the routes and vehicles operated by F.E. Thorpe were acquired by Metroline. Further details of the Dart SLF fleet originating with Thorpe can be found under the Metroline heading.

AJ02ZRY was a solitary Marshall Capital bodied Dennis Dart SLF saloon purchased from Marshalls. It was numbered MLF122. It is captured by the camera passing through Golders Green bus station on route 210 to Brent Cross. *Ian Armstrong Collection*

November 2003 saw the arrival of the final two Pointer Darts with Thorpe. DLF124 (KX53SDU) is seen passing Golders Green bus station on route 210. *Collin Lloyd/Jeff Lloyd Collection*

EPSOM BUSES/ QUALITY LINE

The first Dennis Darts arrived with Epsom Buses during 1993. These Plaxton Pointers were registered K112/3NGK and were put to use on the 498 (Epsom-Croydon) and 562 (Epsom-Weybridge). A third arrived in October 1994 registered M960CGF. The final two step-entrance Pointers arrived in 1995 and were used on the 5 between Epsom and Watersedge. The vehicles in question were registered N401/2SPA. In January 2002 the fleet of Darts gained rolling stock numbers LD12 to LD16.

Epsom Buses was the first operator within the former London Country area to take delivery of the shorter 8.8m MPD. Eleven of the type registered S456-466LGN were delivered during December 1998, taking up stock numbers 456-466, for routes 413 (Morden Station-Sutton), S1 (Hackbridge-Sutton-Banstead) and S5 (Mitcham Common-Wallington) from 4 January 1999. They replaced former London General Optare

K112NGK was the first of two Plaxton Pointer bodied Dennis Darts delivered to Epsom Buses in 1993. It is seen heading towards Chessington, photographed in Epsom. *Collin Lloyd/ Jeff Lloyd Collection*

MetroRiders. They were renumbered SD10 to SD20 in January 2002. Livery of maroon and cream was worn by this batch of vehicles.

Two 10.1m long Pointer Darts arrived in April 1999. 467/8 (T467/8EGT) were taken into stock for use on London route 463 (Coulsdon, Clockhouse Estate-Wallington Station). They replaced a pair of step-entrance Darts which moved on to other routes. The maroon and cream livery were again worn by these vehicles, which also featured air conditioning units.

The contract for the 408 was taken over in January 2000 after it was abandoned by Arriva Southern Counties. MPD V943DNB was taken on loan at this time by Epsom, operating in an all-white livery. It returned off loan in March, only to return in September 2001 for use as a spare vehicle, taking stock number SD22.

The first Alexander ALX200s arrived in March and April, these being for the 408 (Sutton-Cobham) and S3 (Worcester Park Station-Sutton Hospital). Registered W871-6VGT, these were also fitted with air conditioning units.

A four-year-old Dart SLF was taken on loan during April 2000 registered R85XNE. It was used on route 413. A second loan arrived in February 2001 registered W937JNF. This saloon carried an Alexander ALX200 body and was used on Epsom local service E9. It was followed two months later by the loan of a 10.7m long Pointer Dart registered T51JBA, arriving in April 2001. This latter vehicle stayed with Epsom until January 2002, being used on the K50 Kingston Park & Ride service in December 2001. It was used alongside five other 11.3m Super Pointer Darts, these being registered R91/2XNE, S779/82RNE and V897DNB. This quintet arrived in November 2001,

The first low-floor Dennis Dart SLFs arrived with Epsom Buses in December 1998 and were shared between routes S1, S5 and 413. S463LGN was one of the batch which was delivered in the maroon and cream livery. *Ian Armstrong Collection*

April 1999 saw two longer Dart SLFs arrive for the take up of route 463. T467EGT was one of the pair. It is seen at Wallington Station wearing the original livery. *Ian Armstrong Collection*

working alongside similar Alexander ALX200 bodied Dart SLFs Y202KNB and VX51RBO, RCU/V.

Over the autumn of 2001, the majority of the fleet of Dennis Dart SLF saloons lost the maroon and cream livery in favour of the red livery, the fleet name being altered to Quality Line at this time.

The next batch of Dart SLFs arrived in January 2002, these again carrying Alexander ALX200s. SD29 to SD36 (SN51UCM/L/H/J/O/P/R/S) were taken into stock to upgrade the fleet on the S1, displacing the original Pointer MPDs, which were used by Epsom on non-London services in Surrey. A common trait with Epsom Buses Dart SLFs was the fitting of air conditioning units to the vehicles. Most of this batch operated with the company until withdrawal in May 2009. Over the coming years, the Optare Solo was the vehicle of choice, the Dart falling out of favour.

A pair of Pointer Darts were hired in March 2002. VU02TPX/Z were put to use on the 408.

The contract for the 293 was won in July 2003, with Quality Line ordering a fleet of Mercedes-Benz Citaros. The route was taken over early, seeing a handful of Dart SLFs being loaned to the company. This saw the return of VX51RBO, which had previously been hired in 2001. It was joined by Y201KNB, VX51PZM, RBY and RCF. The Citaros were later temporarily withdrawn following fires on the articulated versions in Central London, this led to further Dart hires for a week or so whilst safety inspections were carried out.

A brief resurgence was made by the Dart in July 2005. It was at this time that six East Lancs Myllennium bodied Darts were taken into stock for route S3. They displaced older ALX200s, these being used on country routes. These remained in service until January 2015, with the exception of SD41 which was smoke-damaged in 2014.

Quality Line purchased its first dedicated driver training vehicle in October 2006. It came from Centra London in the form of a Caetano Nimbus bodied Dennis Dart SLF, replacing step-entrance Darts which were being used in this role. It was given fleet number ET1 and was registered HV52WSZ.

The final Darts to be taken into stock were nine East Lancs Esteem bodied ADL Darts. SD43 to SD51 (PE56UFH/J/K/L/M/N/P/R/S) arrived in February 2007.

Quality Line was purchased by the RATP Group on 20 April 2012, after which time the Company came under the same management as London United. It was operated as a separate concern.

Under the ownership of RATP, three Plaxton Pointer bodied Dart SLF saloons were taken into stock during October 2012 from London United. These vehicles were the former DPS539, 597 and 600 (Y539XAG, SN51TDO and SN51TCU). These were put on the 479 to start, before taking up service on the 560. The 560 was a short-term contract operating between Streatham Common Station and Pollards Hill, running between November 2012 and April 2013.

Mitcham finds SD32 (SN51UCJ) heading towards Banstead on the S1. The Quality Line name can be seen prominent on the front of the vehicle. *Collin Lloyd/ Jeff Lloyd Collection*

The Alexander
ALX200s purchased for the S3 were replaced by a new batch of six East Lancs Myllennium bodied ADL Darts. SD42 (PL05PLX) shows off the smart bodywork of these vehicles. It is seen in Sutton heading towards Malden Manor. *Liam Farrer-Beddall*

The final new batch of Darts to be purchased by Epsom Buses/Quality Line arrived in February 2007. SD49 (PE56UFP) is again photographed in Sutton heading towards Mitcham on the S1. *Ian Armstrong Collection*

AIRLINKS

Airlinks was predominantly a coach operator, along with being involved in airside work at Heathrow Airport. The Company commenced operation of service H30 between Hatton Cross, Heathrow Terminal 4, Heathrow Cargo area and Heathrow's Central Area in May 1999. For this service, six Plaxton Pointer bodied Dennis Dart SLFs were purchased. They were registered T71-6WWV and remained on the route until May 2004 when it was withdrawn.

T75WWV represents the small fleet of Pointer Dart SLFs used by Airlinks on the H30. It is seen approaching Heathrow Central bus station on this route. *Colin Lloyd/Jeff Lloyd*

SOVEREIGN, HARROW

Sovereign Bus & Coach was successful in winning a number of LRT tenders in the Harrow area in 1990. This led to the formation of Sovereign (Harrow) Ltd in October 1991, initially using minibuses.

The routes were upgraded in 1999 when no less than fifty-two Plaxton Pointer bodied Dart SLF saloons were taken into stock for use on the Harrow network. Sovereign retained the contracts for routes H10, H11, H13 and H17, as well as winning the contracts for routes 183, 683 and H12 from Metroline. The main batch of single-deckers was numbered 503/4/6-40/2-54/6/7 (T503/4JPP, V506-40/2-54/6/7JBH). They were shared between Harrow and Edgware.

Five 9.3m Dart SLFs were acquired for use on the H17, arriving in September. These single-doored saloons were numbered 558 to 562 (V558-62JBH) and were added to Harrow's allocation.

At the end of 2001, the fleet of Dart SLFs on the 183 were replaced by Volvo B7TLs. At this time the 10.1m Dart SLFs moved onto the H17 on which they displaced the shorter 9.3m Dart SLFs on the 398, in turn replacing older Mercedes-Benz minibuses.

Ten of the batch, 540/2-50 (V540JBH etc), were placed on loan to various London operators when the need arose. These are listed under the relevant company headings in this book (Mitcham Belle, F.E. Thorpe, Ealing Community Transport, First London).

French transport group Transdev purchased London Sovereign in November 2002, placing the company under common ownership with London United. Harrow was given garage code SO, whilst Edgware became BT.

By the spring of 2004, a couple of the buses had been involved in accidents and were either written off or repaired. At the same time, 518 (V518JBH) lost its cream, blue and black livery in favour of an all-red livery and received fleet number SDP518. It was shortly followed by 532 and 539, and a grey skirt was also applied. The class code SDP was adopted by the 10.1m long Dart SLFs under their new ownership, rather than fitting in with the DPS class operated by sister company London United. The shorter 9.3m members of the fleet were classified DPF, becoming DPF558-563 respectively.

Again, very little of interest happened to these vehicles for the remainder of their careers in London. SDP539 was sent on loan to Stagecoach London at Bromley for use on the seasonal Park & Ride service. It was placed on loan in November 2005 and remained in use there until the end of December. In January 2006, it went on loan to Metroline, operating from Holloway. A month later it was placed in the care of London United and operated from Shepherd's Bush and Stamford Brook garages until it was transferred back to Sovereign in February 2007.

The DPFs and SDPs continued to operate in the Harrow area under Transdev control until late 2009, early 2010 when the lease for these vehicles expired. The DPF class were the first to leave London, being followed by the SDPs.

SOVEREIGN, HARROW • 159

V512JBH shows off the original Sovereign, Harrow livery. It is photographed at Stanmore Underground Station operating route H12. *Ian Armstrong Collection*

Sovereign replaced midibuses on the 398 in 2001. V560JBH is seen at the Ruislip Station terminus blinded for its return journey to Greenford. *Ian Armstrong Collection*

WINGS BUSES

Wings Buses was one of the smaller London operators, with operations confined to west London. They first took delivery of the Dennis Dart SLF in November 1999 when three 10.3m East Lancs Spryte bodied examples arrived. They wore a mustard yellow livery, complete with an orange roof and red skirt. Registered V336-8MBV, these vehicles were employed on the U7 (Uxbridge-Hayes) and were later numbered WB1 to WB3.

These were followed by a similar batch in March 2000. Numbered WB4 to WB7, these Dart SLFs were registered W435-8CRN, and were put to use on the H50 (Hayes-West Drayton) from April. Again, red was not the livery chosen for these vehicles, instead dark green was chosen, with a light green front end, in a similar style to London & Country.

The final batch of Dart SLFs to operate with Wings arrived in May 2002. These 8.8m Pointer MPDs were registered SK02TZN/O/P/R/S/T/U/V/W/X and remained un-numbered by the Company. This time red was the chosen colour, with a small amount of yellow being applied. This batch was put to use on the E6 between Bull's Bridge and Greenford.

Wings continued to operate these vehicles until March 2004 when they were taken over by Tellings-Golden Miller. The three batches continued to operate under this new company and passed to Travel London in June 2005. With the exception of V336-8MBV, the other two batches then passed to Abellio London in June 2009 and remained in use with them until 2017 and 2018 when they were sold.

Two batches of East Lancs Spryte bodied Dart SLFs were taken into stock by Wings. V338MBV is seen in Uxbridge, completing its journey on route U7. *Collin Lloyd/Jeff Lloyd Collection*

ARRIVA THE SHIRES & ESSEX

Arriva The Shires & Essex operated a large number of Dennis Darts and Dart SLF saloons in their provincial operations in Hertfordshire, Bedfordshire, Buckinghamshire and Essex. A small number of the type were also purchased for use on the Company's London contracts.

The majority of Dennis Dart SLFs operated by Arriva the Shires & Essex carried Plaxton Pointer bodywork. However, nineteen dual-doored 9.4m Alexander ALX200s, 3461-9/7-9/81 (W461XKX etc), were taken into stock by the company during May 2000 for the Arriva East Herts & Essex operation. All were allocated to Harlow's Debden outstation, from where they operated the W13 (Leytonstone-Wanstead-South Woodford-Woodford Wells), W14 (Leyton-Leytonstone-Wanstead-Snaresbrook-South Woodford Station-Woodford Bridge) and 397 (Debden Station-Woodford Wells-Chingford Station-Chingford Mount). They operated in Arriva's national livery of turquoise and cream. Control of Debden depot passed from Arriva the Shires & Essex to Arriva London in March 2005. The nineteen ALX200s transferred to Edmonton and were renumbered ADL61-9, 71-9 and ADL81.

The first Dennis Darts to be purchased for London area services by Arriva the Shires came in the form of low-floor Alexander ALX200s for several routes in north-east London. 3472 (W472XKX) is seen in the original livery worn by the batch, photographed in Debden. *Colin Lloyd/Jeff Lloyd Collection*

A handful of Wright Crusader bodied Dennis Dart SLFs were acquired by Arriva The Shires & Essex in November 1997 from County Bus. Initially allocated to Ware garage, they were used on services between the town and Hertford. In August 2003, 3435, 3439 and 3440 (R165/9/70GNW) transferred across to Debden where they were used on TfL service 549 (South Woodford Station-Roding Valley-Loughton Station). For this, the trio received red livery, the contract for the 549 lasting until February 2005, after which these Dart SLFs were repainted into standard Arriva livery and were reallocated within The Shires group.

The first Plaxton Pointer bodied Dart SLF saloons were purchased by The Shires in 1997. However, it was not until May 2003 that any were put to use on London contracts. 3828 (KE03UKK) was allocated to Ware garage where it was used on the single-vehicle route 327 (Waltham Cross-Turkey Street circular). On Sundays it could be found operating other services from Ware.

An additional three 8.8m Pointer MPDs arrived in December 2003, this time for High Wycombe. 3837 to 3839 (KE53NEU, NFA/C) were stored at Aylesbury until January 2004 when they entered service on the U9 (Uxbridge Station-Harefield West/Hospital).

Routes H18 and H19 were taken over by The Shires in September 1999, as the PVR on the route increased. As a short-term solution, standard liveried Dart SLFs were used by The Shires. At the same time DDL15 (S315JUA) was taken on loan from Arriva London in September 2006. It remained on loan to The Shires until August 2008 when it was officially taken into stock by the company and numbered 3218.

Arriva the Shires took over operation of Uxbridge area service U9 in January 2004 for which three Pointer Darts were purchased. The middle member of the batch, 3838 (KE53NFA), is seen in Uxbridge wearing the 100% red livery. *Ian Armstrong Collection*

A pair of new ADL Pointer Darts was delivered to the Company during December 2006, both being built to dual-door layout. The first was numbered 3804 (SN56AXG) and was put to use on the H18 and H19 respectively, supplementing the fleet of Volvo B6BLEs in use on those services. The second took up rolling stock number 3805 (SN56AXH) and joined similar vehicles on the U9 in the Uxbridge area but was not well received on this service. 3804 was allocated to Garston, whilst 3805 found a home at High Wycombe.

August 2008 saw the arrival of two MPDs from Arriva London, these being the former PDL1 and PDL2 (V421/2DGT). They took up fleet numbers 3226 and 3225, with the former vehicle becoming a spare for the U9, whilst 3225 joined the main fleet and was repainted into standard Arriva livery.

3218 (S318JUA) was joined by sister vehicle DDL17 (S317JUA) in December 2008, which was numbered 3220. This too operated from Garston in the Harrow area. The following years also saw a number of former Arriva London Dart SLFs enter service with Arriva the Shires, being allocated to various garages in the Company.

Two PDLs were transferred from Arriva London to Garston in November 2015. PDL117 and PDL118 (LJ05GOP/U) were the vehicles concerned and were numbered 3802 and 3803 by The Shires. Control of the London operations passed to Arriva London in January 2016, although the fleet continued to operate for a number of months on The Shires Operators' licence.

The final pair of new Pointer Darts were delivered to the company for use on the H18 and H19 in December 2006. 3804 (SN56AXG) is photographed on layover in Harrow showing off its dual-door layout. *Ian Armstrong Collection*

MITCHAM BELLE

Mitcham Belle was another long-established coach operator in the London area. They were successful in winning the tender for the 127 (Purley Station-Tooting Broadway) in April 1999. The 127 itself had been operated by numerous non-red operators since privatisation. A batch of twelve 10.7m Plaxton Pointer bodied Dart SLFs was taken into stock, registered T151-4/6-9OGC and T875-7/80HGT. They entered service wearing a white based livery with a red roof and blue skirt.

Two further services, the 200 (Raynes Park-Mitcham) and 201 (Tulse Hill-Mitcham), were taken over in June 2000. Twenty-four shorter 10.1m Pointer Dart SLFs were taken into stock for the routes. A new base on Beddington Lane was established to house the growing fleet. The batch was registered W112/4/6/7-9/22/4/6-8/32-4/6-8/41-4/6/7/9WGT. One of this batch was used on temporary service 407A (Purley-Old Barn Lane), the route introduced as a result of flooding on Arriva London's main 407 service, in December 2000.

Six Pointer Dart SLFs were hired from Sovereign and Dawson Rentals in November & December 2001 for route 152 (Pollards Hill-New Malden), after the route was won from London General, along with an extension of route 201 to Morden Station. Those from Dawson Rentals were registered S405TMB, W671TNV and W681TNV; these were

T158OGC was part of the first batch of Pointer Darts purchased by Mitcham Belle for use on route 127, the first London contract to be won by the company. It is seen at Pollards Hill operating route 152 towards New Malden. *Ian Armstrong Collection*

mostly used on the 127. Those from Sovereign were registered V540/2-50JBH, arriving in December. Three additional Dart SLFs were hired to cover the extension of the 201 in December. R530/2YRP carried Wright Crusader bodies, whilst T674TSG carried Alexander ALX200 bodywork. These hired Dart SLFs were used on the 127, allowing native Darts to move to the 152.

New rolling stock for the 152 came in the form of the Caetano Nimbus bodied Dart SLF. Caetano demonstrator X93FOR was loaned in January and February 2002 before the batch arrived. The new rolling stock began to arrive in February, these being the first new vehicles to be numbered into a numbering sequence, these being 053 to 061 (KM51BFO/U/X/L/P/N/V/Y). 062-065 (KM51BEO and KU02YEA-C) followed in March. Delivery was complete in April when 066-069 (KU02YBD-G) were taken into stock. After this time, the hired Dart SLFs returned off loan.

Fourteen Caetano Nimbus bodied Dart SLFs arrived in November 2002. Registered HV52WSJ-L/N/O/U/W/X/Y/Z, WTA/G/J/K, these vehicles were numbered 070 to 083. They were put to use on newly won service 493 between Richmond and Tooting, St Georges Hospital.

The Caetano Nimbus saloons proved to be unreliable, leading to the loan of two Pointer Dart SLFs from Go-Ahead London. LDP74 and LDP78 arrived with the company on 22 September 2003, remaining in use until January 2004. The final Dart SLF to arrive with the fleet arrived in January 2004 registered KX53SHJ. Rolling stock number 84 was allotted to this vehicle.

Mitcham Belle continued to operate until August 2004 when the Company was acquired by Centra London. Further details of this operator can be found later in this book.

New rolling stock for the 152 arrived in the opening months of 2002. KM51BFN is seen at Pollards Hill on its intended route. *Ian Armstrong Collection*

CONNEX

Connex was new to the UK operation in July 1999, establishing a garage at Beddington Cross. The first Dennis Darts entered the fleet in February 2000 when three Carlyle Dartlines arrived. DT1, DT25 and DT41 were put to use on rail replacement work.

Route 322 (Crystal Palace-Elephant & Castle) was taken on by Connex in April, with a batch of Alexander ALX200 bodied Dart SLFs being ordered. A delay in the arrival of these vehicles led to the loan of a number of Pointer MPDs. Four were numbered DP60/2-4 and carried registration marks V260BNV, W362-4ABD. They were joined by W921/2JNF, T73JBA, V943DNB, W936/7JNF. They were loaned for four months before being returned. T674TSG, an Alexander ALX200, was also loaned at this time for use in the Lewes area.

The intended batch of ALX200s for the 322 arrived in June 2000. These were numbered DA1 to DA14 (W601-09MWJ, C8NEX, W610-4MWJ), displacing the hired

The late arrival of new rolling stock for the 322 led to the loan of a number of Dennis Dart SLF saloons. W362ABD was one of these and is seen at Elephant & Castle. *Colin Lloyd/ Jeff Lloyd Collection*

Dart SLFs. These carried a red livery with a dark blue skirt and yellow line and were allocated to Beddington Cross. DP62 and DP63 were retained by Connex and used on a service between Lewes and Uckfield, operating alongside older Carlyle Dartlines.

Arriva London subcontracted route 315 (Balham-Norwood) to Connex in December 2000. DP62 and DP63, mentioned above, were used on this service, along with a number of hired Dart SLFs, these being numbered DP64 and DP65, these having already been hired by Connex as DP64 and DP60 mentioned above. An additional Pointer Dart was loaned registered T546HNH, joining the others on the 315. The hired Dart SLFs mentioned above that gained DP class codes remained in operation with Connex during 2001 and early 2002 before being sold. DP62 was retained and repainted red in July 2002.

Four new ALX200s for the 315 were delivered in April 2001. These carried on from the 2000 delivery, numbered DA15-8 (Y215EWF, Y116-8HWB).

Route 405 (West Croydon-Redhill) was taken over in April 2001. Four 10.7m Pointer Dart SLFs were purchased for the route, numbered DPL11-14 (Y211-4HWJ). These were new to Manchester Airport, also seeing service with Bus Eireann before arriving in London. DP62/3 were also transferred to the route.

July 2001 saw the operations of Limebourne Travel (Independent Way) acquired by Connex. A fleet of thirty-four Caetano Compass bodied Dart SLFs were taken into stock, all operating from a base in Battersea (QB). Routes 42, 156 and 344 were operated by these vehicles. Rolling stock numbers DCL401 to DCL437 (with gaps) were allocated to the batch. A repaint programme commenced in September, the Dart SLFs losing their green skirts. Six step-entrance Carlyle Dartline bodied Darts were also acquired, these retaining fleet numbers DT125/6, 134/6, 142 and 157. These were used on the C3 and were again allocated to Battersea.

The new rolling stock for the 322 arrived in June 2000. DA14 (W614MWJ) shows off the original Connex London livery and is followed by DA6 (W606MWJ). *Ian Armstrong Collection*

Connex was the third operator of Y213HWJ, which took stock number DPL13. It is photographed at West Croydon bus station about to head to Redhill on the 405, taken over at short notice from Arriva. *Ian Armstrong Collection*

The Caetano Compass bodied Dennis Dart SLF saloons inherited from Limebourne Travel were not liked by Connex with many being sold off. However, some were retained by Connex for driver training duties. DCL422 (T422LGP) is seen in this guise at Trafalgar Square. *David Beddall*

The G1 (Streatham High Road-Battersea) was taken over by Connex in January 2002. Twelve 8.8m MPDs were taken into stock for the route. Numbers DP1-12 were allotted to the batch, these carrying registration plates YT51DZY/Z, EAA/C/E/F/G/J/K/M/O/P. DP1 arrived in December 2001, the rest arriving in January 2002.

The Caetano Compass bodied Dart SLFs were unpopular with Connex and did not last long with the company. The 156 and 344 had double-deck operation. The 42 was soon lost to Durham Travel Services (DTS), originally due to transfer in April 2002, but was taken over early in January. DCL404/6, 421/2/4-6 were placed on loan with the latter operator to cover for the late arrival of Scania singles. Most of the type departed in 2002, others being transferred to driver training vehicles.

The rolling stock on the 322 and G1 was swapped between the routes in September 2003. The MPDs used on the G1 moved across to Battersea along with the route in January 2004.

A month later, in February 2004, the National Express Group purchased the operations and vehicles of Connex, coming under the control of Travel London.

HACKNEY COMMUNITY TRANSPORT

Hackney Community Transport provides a number of mobility services on behalf of London Buses Limited, along with community buses in East London. Route 153 (Liverpool Street Station-Finsbury Park) was the first London service to be won by the company. Eleven 10.5m Caetano Nimbus bodied Dart SLFs were taken in to stock at Ash Grove, sharing the garage with East Thames Buses. Registration marks X584-9/91-5ORV were carried by these vehicles, which were numbered HDC1-11. Caetano demonstrator X93FOR was also loaned before their arrival. HDC1-11 were joined by HX51LPE, acquired from White Rose in November 2002.

Route 394 had been operated by a fleet of Renault Rohill minibuses since September 2001. In April 2003, the route was renewed, being upgraded to nine Caetano Slimbus bodied Dart SLFs. These were registered KV03ZFE-H, HX03MGV/U/J/Y/Z, taking stock numbers DCS1-9. The route originally ran between Islington and Cambridge Heath, later being extended to Homerton Hospital.

The Caetano Nimbus became the preferred choice of bodywork for the first two batches of Dart SLFs purchased by Hackney Community Transport. HDC1 (X584ORV) was one of eleven taken into stock for route 153. *Ian Armstrong Collection*

In October 2003, the need for an extra vehicle on the 153 arose. This was fulfilled by former Connex London DPL14 (Y214HWJ), taken on loan for a short period, leaving London during 2004.

The company took up the new name CT Plus in December 2005. Three former Limebourne Caetano Compass Dart SLFs were acquired in October 2005. T432, 431, 433LGP were numbered HDC12-14. HDC13 was used to cover the increase on the 153, the others were used as driver trainers.

In the spring of 2007, route W13 (Leytonstone-Woodford Wells) was won by CT Plus. A fleet of seven ADL Enviro 200/East Lancs Esteem saloons were taken into stock by the company. The late arrival of these vehicles meant that five Caetano Nimbus bodied Darts needed to be hired from Dawson Rentals. HDC14-18 were loaned between April and July 2007, these being registered KM51EFO, KU02YBB, KU02YBC, KU02YBD and KU02YBE. They had previously operated with Mitcham Belle and Centra, retaining their red with blue skirt livery.

HDC12 transferred to the main CT Plus fleet, leaving a gap in the training fleet. Two former Docklands Buses Caetano Nimbus bodied Dart SLFs were hired in January and March 2009. The vehicles were registered HV02OZT and HV02PDO.

Five Plaxton Pointer bodied Dennis Dart SLFs were acquired by CT Plus between January 2010 and February 2012, forming a pool of spare vehicles. First to arrive was

Nine shorter
Caetano Slimbus saloons arrived in 2003 for the conversion of route 394 from minibuses. DCS8 (HX03MGY) is seen stopped in Hackney Central.
David Beddall

Three Caetano Compass bodied Dart SLFs were acquired in December 2005. HDC12 (T433LGP) is seen on route 153, passing through Islington. *Collin Lloyd/Jeff Lloyd Collection*

SN53EUD was new to Go-Ahead London and passed to CT Plus in October 2011. It is seen operating the 394 in Hackney. *Liam Farrer-Beddall*

former Go-Ahead London 9.2m Pointer bodied Dart SLF P508RYM. It was leased by CT Plus in January 2010, taking stock number DPS1. Former Abellio London MPD BU05HFG was loaned in October, being given fleet number DPS2. A year passed before any more were acquired. In October 2011, 10.2m long Plaxton Pointer SN53EUD arrived, originating with Go-Ahead London. As this vehicle was longer, it was numbered DP1 rather than in the DPS class. The final pair of Pointer bodied Dart SLFs arrived during February 2012. Numerically, MM51XVB was the first of the pair, being numbered DPS3. It arrived wearing an all-white livery which it retained for its stay with CT Plus in London. It was new to Bodman's of Warminster and was used by CT Plus on both Hospital and Olympic Park contracts. The final Dart SLF to be acquired was numbered DPS4. This was another former Abellio London vehicle which carried registration mark BX54DLK. This kept its red livery and became a spare for TfL work.

DPS4 (BX54DLK) was the final member of the spare pool of vehicles to be acquired. It is seen at Angel Islington heading towards Homerton Hospital. *Liam Farrer-Beddall*

BLUE TRIANGLE

March 2001 saw the arrival of eight Caetano Nimbus bodied Dennis Dart SLF saloons for the 368. DN185 (Y185RCR) was one of this batch and is seen off route at Romford Station. *David Beddall*

Blue Triangle took over route 368 (Barking-Chadwell Heath) from Stagecoach East London in March 2001. The Caetano Nimbus bodied Dart SLF was the chosen vehicle to take over the route, with eight 11.0m long examples being taken into stock. DN181-8 (Y181-8RCR) operated from the company's base in Rainham.

Blue Triangle chose the Plaxton Pointer saloon for other single-deck requirements. The 372 (Hornchurch-Lakeside) was the next service to be taken over, this taking place in January 2003. Four 10.7m long Pointers arrived for this route, being classified DP. Stock numbers DP189 to DP192 were allocated to the batch which took up registration marks EJ52WXC-F, these arriving in December 2002. They were built to single-door layout.

A larger batch of Pointer Dart SLFs was taken into stock in September 2003 for route 66 between Romford Station and Leytonstone. Thirteen of the type arrived numbered DP193 to DP204 (EU53PXY/Z, PYA/B/D/F/G/H/J/L/O/P). These measured the

same length as the previous batch but were built to dual-door layout. These were late arriving, with six Darts being hired to cover for them, along with four Optare Excels loaned from East Thames Buses. S310TMB, T439EBD, T464HNH, P684RWU and P41MLE all carried Plaxton Pointer bodies, whilst R521YRP carried an East Lancs Spryte body. DP189 to DP192 were transferred to route 372 in January 2003.

March 2004 saw the arrival of a solitary Transbus Pointer Dart saloon numbered DP205 (BT04BUS). EU04BVD/F arrived a month later, taking rolling stock numbers DP206 and DP207. They entered the fleet wearing an all-white livery and were purchased for use on rail replacement work. They retained this livery in the autumn of 2005, after which time they received a red livery for use on the 347 between Romford Station and Ockendon Station.

Plaxton Pointer bodied Dart SLF P746HND, which had been used by a number of operators, arrived in September 2004. This 10.6m saloon was built to single-door layout, and wore an all-white livery for use on rail replacement work, as well as providing a spare for route 372. It was sold to Ensign Bus in September 2006 who sold it on for further work.

September 2006 also saw the arrival of two ADL Pointer Darts. Fleet number DP208 was reused for one of the vehicles, along with stock number DP209. Registration marks SN56AYC and AYD were allocated to these vehicles, which were ordered against TfL school route 648. The pair were slightly late in arriving, so existing rolling stock took their place on the service until they had arrived.

The next batch of Dart SLFs did not arrive until December 2002. DP190 (EJ52WXD) was one of four purchased for route 372. It is again seen in Romford off route. *Ian Armstrong Collection*

Route 368 was lost to Docklands Buses in March 2006, making DN181-8 redundant. After this, the batch went on loan to a couple of London operators. In May 2006 they were loaned to Metroline for the take up of route 493 (Richmond-Tooting). The loan ended in October when they moved on to London United, initially used on seasonal service K50, before seeing use on other routes from Hounslow garage, allowing London United's fleet of Dart SLFs to be refurbished.

DN181 and DN188 returned to Blue Triangle in January 2007 and were used on new route 11 between Basildon and Purfleet. They transferred onto the 66 in March, allowing a pair of DPs to move to route 362.

Further members of the batch (DN182/3/6) returned to Blue Triangle in June, with the outstanding members of the batch returned in July 2007. DN183 and 186 did not stay long, going on loan to Eastbourne Buses soon after returning.

In June 2007, Roger Wright sold the operations and a number of buses operated by Blue Triangle to the Go-Ahead Group who kept the Blue Triangle name. The Plaxton Pointer bodied Darts transferred to their new owner, the Caetanos being retained by Roger Wright, forming a pool of loan vehicles under the London Bus Company name.

The newest Darts to be purchased by Blue Triangle arrived in September 2006 for school route 648. These were also used on other services. DP208 (SN56AYC) is seen passing through Romford Town Centre on route 66. *Ian Armstrong Collection*

DURHAM TRAVEL SERVICES

Durham Travel Services (London Easylink) won the contract for the 42 (Liverpool Street Station-Denmark Hill) to start in April 2002. The route was taken on earlier than planned, in January, meaning the new rolling stock was not ready.

Eight Dennis Dart SLFs were hired from Dawson Rentals. Six of these carried East Lancs Spryte bodies, these being registered R519YRP, R524YRP, S399HVV, S551BNV, S401HVV and Y433PBD. Two others carried Plaxton Pointer bodywork, these being registered S395HVV and S397HVV. Fleet numbers DE130-4, DE136, DP135 and DP137 were applied to these vehicles. All operated in an all-white livery, with the exception of S395HVV, which was orange.

Alongside these, seven Caetano Compass bodied Dart SLFs were hired from Connex London, these arriving in February. These were registered T404/6, 421/2/4-7LGP and retained the all-red livery for their stay with Durham Travel Services, with the latter operator's logos being applied to these vehicles. Durham Travel Services collapsed in August, the hired Darts SLFs returning to their rightful owners.

The early takeover of route 42 by Durham Travel Services saw the loan of a number of Dennis Dart SLF saloons with varying bodywork. East Lancs bodied Dart SLF R519YRP is seen entering Liverpool Street bus station in an all-white livery. *Ian Armstrong Collection*

DOCKLANDS BUSES

Docklands Buses has its roots in the Docklands Minibus operations established by Harry Blundred in 1988. The company, as has been mentioned, was acquired by Stagecoach in 1997. Docklands Minibus continued to run operating private hire work and contract work.

The company won the contract for the 167 (Debden-Ilford) in March 2002 at the expense of Arriva London. It was at this time the Company was rebranded as Docklands Buses, opening a new operating centre in Silvertown. Twelve 10.5m Caetano Nimbus bodied Dennis Dart SLF saloons were purchased to operate this new contract. No fleet numbers were carried by these vehicles which were registered HV02OZS/T/U/W/X, PCO/U/X/Y/Z, PDK/O. The red livery was relieved by white and blue fleet names.

Twelve Caetano Nimbus bodied Dart SLFs arrived in March 2002 for the take up of route 167. HV02PCY is captured by the camera in Ilford showing off the Docklands Buses livery. *Jeff Lloyd*

The fleet of Darts proved to be unreliable, with a pair of Optare Solos supporting the services from June 2003. A year later, during the summer of 2004, Stagecoach London loaned Alexander ALX200 bodied Dennis Dart SLF 34295 (Y295FJN) to Docklands to help cover for the native batch.

A second route was won in March 2006, this being for the 368 (Harts Lane Estate-Chadwell Heath). Eight MCV Evolution bodied ADL Darts were ordered for the route. The first three arrived in March registered AE06HCA, HCC and HCD, followed in April by AE06HCF/H/J/K, with the last vehicle arriving in May registered AE06HCG. However, the late arrival of most of the batch led to the loan of 34303-7 (LX51FGA/F/E/D/G) from Stagecoach London, these returning to Stagecoach at the end of April.

Docklands Buses was sold to the Go-Ahead Group in September 2006. As was the case with Blue Triangle, the Docklands Buses name was retained by Go-Ahead, who continued to operate from Silvertown. The company was added to the London General Operators' licence. Further history of the two batches mentioned above can be found under the Go-Ahead London heading.

The MCV Evolution bodied ADL Dart replaced the original fleet of Caetano Nimbus bodied Darts on route 167. AE06HCD is seen on layover in Barking. *Collin Lloyd/Jeff Lloyd Collection*

EAST THAMES BUSES

East Thames Buses was formed by London Buses in 1999 to take over the operations of Harris Bus of Thurrock. With this takeover came routes 108 and 132.

East Thames inherited a fleet of Optare Excel saloons which soon proved to be unreliable. Because of this, a number of Dennis Dart SLF saloons were hired in 2000. Four Dart SLFs arrived in May, two carrying Plaxton Pointer bodies (T553HNH, P942EMS), the other two Wright Crusader bodies (T442/3EBD). T553HNH was operated by the company until July 2001, the others returning off loan much sooner. July 2001 saw the loan of Marshall bodied Dart SLF S721KNV, along with an additional Plaxton Pointer model registered V388SVV.

These latter two vehicles were returned in February 2002, and it was at this time that East Thames acquired two step-entrance Wright Handybus bodied Dennis Dart saloons from London United. These were the former DWL7/8 (JDZ2407/8). T553HNH

July 2001 saw the loan of V388SVV from Dawson Rentals. It was put to use on route 132 for the duration of its stay. *Collin Lloyd/Jeff Lloyd Collection*

put in another appearance and was put to use on the 132 and 108. At the same time, it was numbered DC15. It remained in the fleet until 2005 when it returned off loan.

East Thames Buses took the opportunity to purchase some Caetano Compass bodied Dennis Dart SLF saloons in July 2002. These had previously operated with Limebourne and Connex. Seven in total were purchased, these being DCL428, 430, 433-7 (T428/30/3LGP, V434-7KGF). These also saw service on the 108 and 132 as required.

Durham Travel Services entered liquidation in August 2002, affecting route 42, which was soon taken over by East Thames Buses. Seven additional Caetano Compasses were hired by East Thames Buses, these being the former DCL424-7/9, 431/2 (T424-7/9, 431/2LGP). The increasing need for vehicles on the 42 saw all fourteen of the batch allocated to Ash Grove for use on the 42.

A batch of Scania OmniTowns ordered by Durham Travel Services for route 42 arrived with East Thames Buses in January 2003. This in turn allowed the Caetano Dart SLFs to move from this route on to the 108, displacing Optare Excels which were withdrawn. In March, the fleet of Dart SLFs was renumbered to DC1-14.

The summer of 2004 saw the arrival of a fleet of Wright Cadet saloons. Their arrival meant the demise of the remaining Optare Excels and Dart SLFs.

East Thames Buses was another operator of the Caetano Compass bodied Dennis Dart SLFs that were new to Limebourne. They were acquired in two batches, the first arrived for use on the 108 and 132. DC12 (V434KGF) is seen on the 108 departing Lewisham. *Ian Armstrong Collection*

EALING COMMUNITY TRANSPORT

Ealing Community Transport was another operator of welfare minibuses in London. As the name suggests, their main operating area was the London Borough of Ealing. In 2003 they put a successful bid in for route 195 (Charville Lane Estate-Ealing Hospital). Thirteen 10.5m Caetano Nimbus bodied Transbus Dart saloons were purchased for this route. The batch carried registration marks KX03HZN/P/T/U/V/S/W/Z/R/Y/E/G/F and was allotted rolling stock numbers 101 to 113. They wore a simple livery of all-red, with a lime-green band, complete with yellow/green logos.

Ealing Community Transport took over route 195 in April 2003. The route was operated by a batch of thirteen Caetano Nimbus bodied Dart SLFs. 110 (KX03HZY) was one of these showing off the unique livery of the Company as it approaches Hayes and Harlington station. *Jeff Lloyd Collection*

Like other operators, the delivery of these new Darts was delayed. To fill the gap, five Pointer Darts were hired from Mitcham Belle (544/5/7/9/50-V544JBH etc), originating with Sovereign. All but two arrived in April, these arriving in May.

An extra vehicle was required for the route in 2004 leading to the hire of Pointer Dart SLF W568JVV in March. It was retained by the company until the summer of 2005, getting fleet number 114. Its replacement arrived in July 2005 in the form of another Caetano Nimbus saloon, this time carrying the ADL Dart chassis.

115 (KX05KFW) arrived with the Company during July 2005 and received the standard livery worn by 101-113.

Little happened to the fleet over the following years. The route was extended from Ealing Hospital to Brentford in April 2008, with Ealing Community Transport requiring three additional vehicles. These came in the form of a trio of former Docklands Buses Caetano Nimbus bodied Dart SLFs, acquired through Dawson Rentals. HV02OZU, OZX and PCO were the three Dart SLFs acquired, taking up stock numbers 116 to 118.

Like other London buses, the fleet received ibus equipment in August 2008. However, less than a year later, in March 2009, Ealing Community Transport transferred the route to First London, making the seventeen Nimbus bodied Darts redundant, after which time they passed to Dawson Rentals.

TRAVEL LONDON

The first new Darts to arrive with Travel London were twenty Pointer Darts for the 100. DP116 (BX54DLN) is seen passing St Paul's Cathedral heading towards the southern terminus at Elephant & Castle. *Ian Armstrong Collection*

Travel London was the name adopted by the National Express Group in March 2004 after they re-entered the London bus market by purchasing Connex Bus on 26 February 2004. The opening fleet comprised a number of Dennis Dart SLFs inherited from Connex. Eighteen carried Alexander ALX200 bodies and were numbered DA1-18 (W601-9MWJ, C8NEX, W611-4MWJ, Y215HWF and Y116-8HWB). A similar number of Caetano Compass bodied Dart SLFs were also taken into stock registered T401-4/6-10/3-8/21-3LGP, which took up rolling stock numbers DCL401-23 matching the registrations. The final batch acquired comprised twelve 8.8m Pointer MPDs (DP1-12 - YT51DZY/Z, EAA/C/E/F/G/J/K/M/O/P).

September 2004 saw the arrival of the first new rolling stock. These came in the form of twenty dual-doored 9.3m ADL Pointer Darts. Numbered DP101 to DP120

(BX54DKA/D/E/F/J/K/L/O/U/V/Y, DLD/F/J/K/N/O/U/V/Y), the batch was allocated to Walworth where they were used on the 100 between Shadwell Station and Elephant & Castle. An all-over red livery was worn by these vehicles complete with a white roof.

These were followed in October by eight 8.8m Pointer MPDs for route P13 (Streatham Garage-New Cross Gate). These were also allocated to Walworth, taking up stock numbers DP13-20 (BX54DLZ, DME/F/O/U/V/Y/Z).

The first of two batches of 8.8m MPDs were delivered in April 2005. DP21 to DP30 (BU05HDO/V/X/Y, HEJ, HFA-D/G) were used on the G1 (Streatham High Road-Battersea), displacing DA1-14 from the route. They moved on to sister company Travel West Midlands in May. This batch was allocated to the former Limebourne garage in Battersea.

A further nine MPDs were delivered to Travel London in May. DP31-9 (BU05HFK/M/N/T/V/W/X/Y/Z) were purchased to replace Optare Solos inherited from Connex on the C1 (Victoria and Kensington High Street). The change-over took place in June, and joined those used on the G1 at Battersea.

Travel London's presence in West London and Surrey was significantly increased in June 2005 when the operations of Tellings-Golden Miller were acquired. This brought with it three garages at Fulwell, Byfleet and Hayes, along with a number of services. A large number of Dart SLFs were taken into stock at this time.

Seven step-entrance Dennis Darts were taken into stock, five with Plaxton Pointer bodies, and two with Northern Counties bodywork. Those bodied by Plaxton were numbered 16 (1816MW); 19 (4019MW); 25 (8325MW); 39 (7639MW) and 48 (5948MW); whilst those bodied by Northern Counties were numbered 35 and 67 (1335MW and 4967MW).

Buckingham Palace Road, Victoria finds DP39 (BU05HFZ). It is seen heading towards High Street Kensington on route C1. *Colin Lloyd/Jeff Lloyd Collection*

The low-floor Dennis Dart SLFs carried a mixture of bodywork, the Caetano Nimbus, Plaxton Pointer and East Lancs Spryte. Those carrying Caetano Nimbus bodies were numbered 193 (X93FOR), 421-33 (RA51KKF-H, KKD/E, KLE, KGE, RL02FOT/U, FVM/N, ZTB/C), 446 (GM03TGM), 458-463 (HX04HTP/T/U/V//Z) and 613-33 (RN52EOE/D/C/B/V/W/X, ERO/V/U/K/L, FRF, FPC/A/D, FVR/S, FXD, FYO, FZA). The East Lancs Spryte models were numbered 451 to 457 (V336-8MBV, W435-8CRN).

The Plaxton Pointer model dominated the fleet, with various lengths being taken into stock. The 8.8m Pointer MPDs were numbered in the 300 series, the longer 10.1m variant in the 400s, with the 10.6m and 10.7m being numbered in the 500s and 600s. 301-9 (V301-9MDP, 311-5/7/9/20-4, X311-5/7/9KRX, X371CUY, KP51SXY, X322KRX, 1068MW and RA51KVS), along with 325 to 335 (KN52NFO/P/R/T/U/V/X/Y/C/D/E). Solitary MPD Y38YVV was numbered 338, whilst KV03ZFM/N/P/R/S/T/U/W/X/Y carried fleet numbers 339 to 348. The final batch was new to Wings, numbered 349 to 358 (SK02TZN/O/P/R/S/T/U/V/W/X). The 10.1m variants were grouped in two batches, these being 401-20 (W401-4/7-9/11-3UGM, RX51FGG/K/J/M/N/O/P) with gaps; and 434-445 (KM02HFP/R/S/T/U/V, RD02BJK/O/U/V/X/Z). The only 10.6m Pointer Darts were numbered 501 to 510 (R501-10SJM) and 520 (N305DHE). Numerically, the final two batches to be acquired were the 10.7m models. These were numbered 515-9 (S515-7JJH, S518/9TCF) and 601-9/11/2 (W601-9/11/2UJM). The fleet soon got new fleet names, with the Darts used on London contracts being repainted.

342-5 transferred to Byfleet in September 2005, receiving a white and red livery soon after. They joined similar 339 to 341 which had transferred there in January 2005, just before Tellings-Golden Miller was acquired.

Former Connex Alexander ALX200s DA15-18 got new fleet numbers DA5 to DA8 in May 2006. It was at this time that Travel London lost the 315, the route that they had been operating for a number of years. After this time, DA5-7 moved to Fulwell and joined the fleet of Mercedes-Benz Vario minibuses on the H20, H26 and H28. At the same time DA8 was reallocated to Byfleet and used on the service to Wisley Gardens. DA7 and DA8 were returned to the main London fleet in late 2006, DA7 initially at Battersea before joining DA8 at Beddington.

Travel London was successful in winning the tender for route 152 (New Malden-Pollards Hill) which started in April 2006. The route was taken up by the former Wings East Lancs bodied Dart SLFs W435-8CRN, along with former silver Pointer Dart 503 (R503SJM). The East Lancs Darts had come off the H50 in March and were sent to Travel West Midlands' Walsall garage for a full repaint into red, returning to Beddington Cross in April.

Six Pointer bodied Dart SLFs were hired from Stagecoach London for use on the 152, working alongside the East Lancs Darts. 34119-123 (V119/20, 174, 122/3MVX) and 34196 (W196DNO) took up stock numbers DP479-83 and DP478 with Travel London in June 2006. 34196 was first to be returned to Stagecoach in August, the others leaving in September, moving onto Stagecoach Warwickshire rather than going back to Stagecoach London. They were replaced by DP434-440 after the loss of route 203 to London United in September.

June 2006 saw the former Tellings-Golden Miller fleet renumbered into the Travel London series. Plaxton Pointers gained the DP class code; those carrying the East Lancs Spryte body were classified DE; whilst the Caetano Nimbus bodied Dart SLFs were classified DC. The renumbering was as follows:

301-9 to DP41-9; 311-5 to DP51-5; 317, 323, 319, 320 to DP57-60, 322, 338, 321, 324 to DP61-4; 349-358 to DP65-74; 325-335 to DP75-85; 39-348 to DP86-95; 401-4/7-9/11-3 to DP401 etc; 414, 416, 415, 417-20 to DP434-40; 434-45 to DP441-452; 501-10 to DP701-10; 520 to DP711; 515-9 to DP715-9; 601-9/11/12 to DP721-9/31/2; 451-7 to DE414-20; 93 to DC433; 427, 424, 425, 421-3, 426 to DC453-9; 428-33 to DC460-5; 446 to DC466; 458-463 to DC467-472; 616, 615, 614, 613, 617-20 to DC733-740; 622, 621, 623, 624, 627, 626, 628, 625, 629-633 to DC741-753.

Walworth took delivery of five 10.1m dual-doored Pointers for use on the 129 (Greenwich, *Cutty Sark*-North Greenwich) in May 2006. Registration marks LF06YRJ-N were allocated to these vehicles, which took up rolling stock numbers DP473-7.

Byfleet's route 441 gained a fleet of four Pointer MPDs in September 2006. DP1 to DP4 (LJ56ONH/K/L/M) wore the white and red Surrey area livery and were branded for the service. The batch also featured air conditioning. DP702/4/5 were displaced from the 441. DE420 acted as a spare vehicle for the route, this vehicle being given the same livery as DP1-4. The displaced vehicles were used by Travel London on the Kingston University contract over the Christmas 2006 period. They had been due to depart to Travel West Midlands but were rejected, these then remained at Fulwell. The transfer of the trio led to the cascade of DP715-7 to Byfleet for further service.

March 2007 saw the renumbering of the Travel London fleet into a four-digit system, similar to that used by the National Express Group in the West Midlands and Dundee. The Alexander ALX200s DA5-8 became 8005-8. Caetano Nimbus bodied DC433 was renumbered 8433, whilst similar DC453-472 became 8453-72, and DC733-53 took up fleet numbers 8733-53. The East Lancs Spryte bodied Dart SLFs DE414-20 were renumbered 8414-20. Finally, the Plaxton Pointer bodied Dennis Dart SLFs were renumbered as follows; DP1-4 became 8001-4; DP11/3-39/41-9/51-5/7-95 were renumbered 8011 etc. 8301-20 were the new identities taken up by DP101-20. DP401-4/7-9/11-3 became 8401 etc. DP434-452 took up new rolling stock numbers 8434-52.

April 2006 saw six Plaxton Pointer bodied Dart SLFs hired by Travel London from Stagecoach London for use on the 152. W196DNO, Stagecoach's 34196, carried fleet number DP478 whilst operating with Travel London. *Ian Armstrong Collection*

Five ADL Pointer Darts were purchased for route 129, allocated to Walworth. DP474 (LF06YRK) is photographed on Millennium Way, North Greenwich heading for the *Cutty Sark. Jeff Lloyd Collection*

DP473-7 were given new fleet numbers 8473-7. The final batch, DP701-11/5-9/21-9/31/2, was renumbered 8701 etc.

Just prior to the renumbering, 506 to 510 (R506-10SJM) were repainted in the white and red Surrey livery, being reallocated to Byfleet from where they operated routes 218, 451, 461, 566 and 567.

Plaxton Pointer MPD bodied Dart SLF 8058 (1068MW) was re-registered in April 2007. At this time, the vehicle gained new registration mark Y864KTF, 1068MW being returned to Tellings-Golden Miller.

May 2007 saw the loss of the E6 meaning that 8065-74 were surplus to requirements. At this time, the H28 moved to Fulwell, with this batch seeing service on the route for a short period of time. Once the original batch of Dart SLFs used on the H28 moved across to Fulwell, 8065-74 transferred to Byfleet in August.

Six Pointer MPDs were added to the Travel Surrey fleet in June 2007, being acquired from Flights Hallmark. At this time, Byfleet took delivery of 8009/10 (Y37, 42YVV) and 8096-99 (YT51DZZ, EAA, EAJ and EAP) for routes 426 (Staines-Woking), 446 (Staines-Woking), 451 (New Haw-Staines) and 513 (Kingston-Downside), alongside school routes 663 and 664.

June 2007 also saw the H28 move once again, this time to Hayes garage. 8051-5/7/9/61 made the move as well, by which time they had received the 100 per cent red livery.

April 2008 was when a 10.7m long Dennis Dart SLF registered KP51UFK was delivered. It was hired to cover for the late arrival of an Enviro 300 saloon at Byfleet, being used on routes 472 and 690 until May 2008.

Route 434 (Coulsdon-Whytleafe South) was taken over by Travel London in August 2008. New rolling stock was not received on time, resulting in 8065-7 transferring from Byfleet to Beddington Cross, receiving an all-red repaint. Once the new rolling stock arrived the trio were put to use as iBus floats around Travel London, returning to Byfleet by February 2009.

At the end of the year, in December, Travel London hired six Caetano Nimbus bodied Dennis Dart SLFs from Dawson Rentals, these vehicles previously having operated with Docklands Buses. HV02OZS, PCU/X/Z, PDK/O were the vehicles concerned. They were garaged at Fulwell for the duration of their stay, being mostly used on the H25. They were hired to cover for Travel London's own Darts whilst they were fitted with ibus equipment. They returned off lease in January 2009.

The National Express Group sold Travel London in May 2009 to NedRailways. In October, the Company was rebranded as Abellio London and Abellio Surrey.

Non-London route 441 gained four air-conditioned Pointer MPD saloons. They wore a red and white livery as did all buses allocated to Byfleet. 8002 (LJ56ONK) is seen on layover at Heathrow Central bus station wearing route branding. *Ian Armstrong Collection*

CENTRA LONDON

Centra London had been operating for a number of years under the name of Central Parking Systems with a focus on airport work at Heathrow and Luton. In October 2003, the Company ventured into local bus work in Surrey after acquiring the business of Thames Bus.

The first route to be taken over in the area of study was the 516 (Epsom-Dorking). For this, three 8.8m Pointer MPDs (T546HNH, W361ABD and KV51KZC) were taken into stock during February 2004. The first vehicle had previously operated on loan to Armchair, the second with Connex for their Sussex operations. They wore an all-white livery, with the latter two vehicles being branded for the service. A second route that entered the Greater London area was added in April 2004 when the operations of Stansted-based Locallink were acquired. The route concerned was the 520, running between Loughton and Romford.

The operations and vehicles of Mitcham Belle were purchased by Centra in August 2004. The fleet of Dart SLFs operated by Mitcham Belle at this time needed a lot of attention. This led to the 127 and 200 gaining double-deck operation, supported by a fleet of hired Dart SLFs, this arriving from Dawson Rentals or Ensign Bus. These came in the form of members of the Caetano Compass bodied Dart SLF fleet originating with Limebourne. T401-3, 413/4LGP were hired from Ensign Bus, passing to Dawson Rentals in the spring of 2005. Marshall bodied Dart SLF P830BUD was hired from Dawson Rentals in September, along with similar Plaxton Pointer bodied R439FTU.

To summarise, the fleet of Dart SLFs inherited from Mitcham Belle were T151-9OGC, T875-7/80HGT, W112/4/6-9/22/4/6-8/32-4/6-8/41-4/6/7/9WGT, KM51BFO/U/X/L/P/N/V/Y, KM51BEO, KU02YBA-G, HV52WSJ/K/L/N/O/U/W/X/Y/Z, WTA/G/J/K and KX53SHJ.

Go-Ahead London's LDP19 (P719RYL) and former Connex London DPL14 (Y214HWJ) were also loaned to Centra alongside these Dart SLFs, the latter vehicle being purchased by Centra in October 2004.

The Mitcham Belle Dart SLFs received fleet number prefixes, with DP or DC being applied depending on body type. These class codes were also applied to the other Centra vehicles at the same time. The fleet were repainted in a new livery of all-red with a blue skirt and silver flashes between takeover and June 2005.

August 2005 saw the Heathrow, Gatwick and New Haw operations of Centra sold to Flights Hallmark, owned by the Rotala Group. The former Mitcham Belle operation was retained under the Centra London name, operating from a base in Beddington. However, Centra London was short-lived, losing all of its tenders in the London area. The 127 was first to go in December 2005, with other routes being lost between February and May 2006. After this, the fleet was sold.

W126WGT shows the basic red and blue livery used by Centra London. It is photographed at Southfields. *Ian Armstrong Collection*

NCP CHALLENGER

National Car Parks entered the London bus market in 2005 after winning the contracts for routes 33 (Hammersmith-Fulwell) and 419 (Richmond-Hammersmith) from London United. Both started on the 12 November 2005, using the name NCP Challenger. The Company set up a new operating base in Twickenham.

The route was operated by a fleet of twenty-seven 10.1m ADL Pointer Darts. Fleet numbers NCP01-27 were allocated to these vehicles, which were registered SN55HKD/E/FG/H/J/K/L/M/O/P/T/U/V/W/X/Y, SN55HSD/E, HKZ, HLA/C, SN55DVR/T/U/V/W. An all-red livery was worn relieved by yellow fleet names.

The operations transferred to Transdev in November 2009, being placed under the care of London United. The fleet of Dart SLFs transferred along with a fleet of Optare Versas.

Both of NCP Challenger's Dart routes served the Hammersmith area. NCP10 (SN55HKO) is seen crossing Hammersmith Bridge bound for Fulwell on route 33. *Ian Armstrong Collection*

EAST LONDON BUS GROUP

Stagecoach sold its London operations on 23 June 2006 to Australian bank Macquarie. The sale was complete on 30 August 2006, and from that date the East London Bus Group name was used by the new owners. The sale reintroduced the East London and Selkent fleet names and logos, these being worn by the vehicles. The five-digit fleet numbering scheme introduced by Stagecoach in 2003 was retained, and the fleet was not renumbered.

Many of the early Dennis Dart SLFs purchased by Stagecoach had been cascaded to other Stagecoach operations around the country by 2006. However, a large number of the type were still present in the fleet. These vehicles were numbered 34117, 34147-50/2/6-9, 34161-181, 34190/6, 34198-211, 34222-397, 34551-560, details of registrations can be found under the Stagecoach London section of this book.

The operations north of the river were named East London as demonstrated by 34305 (LX51FGE). It is seen approaching journey's end at Romford Station.
Liam Farrer-Beddall

Four Alexander ALX200 bodied Dennis Dart SLFs, 34272 to 34275, were placed on loan with London United at Hounslow in October 2006. They were loaned to allow London United's own fleet of Plaxton Pointer bodied Dart SLFs to undergo refurbishment. These returned to East London during 2007.

The arrival of seventy-five ADL Enviro 200 saloons between 2006 and 2010 caused the sale of many of the early Dart SLF saloons. The majority initially went to Ensign Bus before being sold on to independent operators for further service.

Stagecoach purchased the East London and Selkent operations in October 2010, bringing the Company back under the Stagecoach London name. A number of Dennis Dart SLFs still survived and over the coming years, they were replaced by newer rolling stock.

East London Bus Group inherited a large number of Plaxton Pointer bodied Dart SLFs from Stagecoach London. 34388 (LX03BZW) was one allocated to Catford at this time. It is seen wearing a basic red livery at Lewisham Station. *Liam Farrer-Beddall*

ABELLIO LONDON

NedRailways acquired the business of Travel London and Travel Surrey on 9 June 2009, being rebranded as Abellio London and Abellio Surrey on 30 October 2009. The fleet of low-floor Darts taken into stock were numbered 8001-8, 8010, 8013-20, 8021-39, 8041-9, 8051-9, 8061/2/4, 8065-99, 8301-20, 8401-13, 8417-20, 8434-40, 8441-8452, 8453-8472, 8473-7, 8708/18/19, 8721-32 and 8733-53. Registrations and body types can be found under the Travel London and Tellings-Golden Miller headings earlier in this book. By 2009, the Dart chassis had been replaced by the Enviro 200 model, this type being the chosen model for fleet replacement.

Abellio London took delivery of a number of second-hand Darts from various dealers, these arriving between 2010 and 2017. The first arrived in February 2010 when ten Pointer Darts, dating back to 2002/3, entered the fleet from Dawson Rentals. KP02PWV, PVE, PUK, PVU and PUJ took up fleet numbers 8478-81/3. Similar KM02HGF/E took delivery numbers 8482 and 8484. KU52YKO/R/S made up the other three, these taking stock numbers 8485 to 8487. They were allocated to Fulwell

Other than those acquired from Travel London, the first Dart SLFs to be acquired by Abellio London arrived in early 2010. 8478 (KP02PWV) represents the batch and is seen passing Hounslow bus station on route 235. *Liam Farrer-Beddall*

where they replaced Caetano Nimbus bodied Darts on the 235. 8478-84 were new to Armchair, whilst 8485-7 originated with F.E. Thorpe. The batch took a while to be repainted and enter service. At the same time KP02PUF, PVK, PVN and PWN were hired from Dawson Rentals for use on temporary route 545.

Two 10.1m Pointer Darts arrived in April from London United Registered SN51SXK (DPS566) and SN51SZF (DPS571), these were allocated to Battersea and Fulwell. They took up fleet numbers 8901/2, being put to use as driver training vehicles.

Fourteen East Lancs Myllennium bodied ADL Darts were acquired by Abellio London in August 2010, replacing a fleet of MPDs at Byfleet. They were owned by Surrey County Council, previously operating with First Berkshire on school services in Surrey. The vehicles were numbered 8761-3 (LK55ACX, ADU, ADV), 8764-71 (LK06BWC/D, LK56JKE/F/J/N/O/V) and 8772-4 (LK07CBF, CBV, CBX). They were repainted into the white and red livery before entering service on routes 446, 458, 461 and 566/7. 8041 to 8049 (V301-9MDP) were also transferred to the country area operations at Byfleet in August 2010.

Two batches of Darts were acquired in 2011. Twelve Caetano Nimbus bodied Dart SLFs originating with Ealing Community Transport or Metrobus were acquired. The former Ealing Community Transport vehicles were numbered 8488-4/9 (KX03HZF/R/S/T/V/Y/Z and KX05KFW). The former Metrobus saloons were registered KX04HRD/E/F/G and originated with Tellings-Golden Miller. These latter four vehicles were numbered 8495-8. 8489/90/2/4 were taken into stock during September, whilst 8491/3/9 arrived in February 2012. 8495-8 followed in March.

The second batch arrived from Volant Passenger Vehicle Services. All nine carried Plaxton Pointer bodywork. The first pair took up rolling stock numbers 8110 and 8111, registered SN04EGD and EFJ. 8112 was next and was registered DK04SUU. 8113/4 carried registration marks KX06LYS/T and arrived in December. KX56HCZ was numbered 8115 by the Company, whilst MX56HYR and HYS were numbered 8116 and 8117. The ninth example had previously operated with Abellio, and was registered BU05HFN, regaining fleet number 8033. 8113 to 8115 arrived in November and were allocated to Hayes for use on the U9, recently won from Arriva the Shires. The others

April 2010 saw the arrival of two former London United Pointer Darts, both of which were put to use as driver training vehicles. 8902 (SN51SZF) is seen having just crossed Putney Bridge. *Liam Farrer-Beddall*

arrived in December and were allocated to Fulwell for use on the H20, although they could be found on any of the single-deck routes operated from this garage.

The next Dart arrived from Dawson Rentals in February 2014. 8435 (RX51FGJ) re-entered the fleet to help cover service increases.

September 2014 saw the loss of the 100 to Go-Ahead London. The late arrival of new rolling stock for the latter operator led to the loan of 8302-10/8 to Go-Ahead. They operated from Go-Ahead London's Mandela Way garage. The Darts returned off loan at the end of the year, with many leaving London during May 2015. 8303 (BX54DKE) returned to Abellio in December 2015. 8003/4 (LJ56ONL/M) also re-entered the fleet in October 2017.

Abellio operated some of the last Dennis Dart SLFs in the London area. During 2020, they were down to three in service, these being 8020/4/37. They were finally withdrawn in April 2020, although 8024 made a brief resurgence on the K1 in June 2020. 8020 and 8024 were finally withdrawn in July. It was at this time that driver trainers 8744 to 8748 were also withdrawn and sold.

The Covid-19 pandemic of 2020/2021 created the need for extra capacity for crew rest rooms. Pointer MPD 8037 (BU05HFX) was used as a rest room at Putney Bridge Station.

A large number of the Pointer MPD fleet at Byfleet were replaced by larger East Lancs Myllennium bodied ADL Darts in August 2010. 8772 (LK07CBF) is seen wearing branding for route 441 when photographed at Staines bus station. *Liam Farrer-Beddall*

Croydon finds 8494 (KX03HZZ), new to Ealing Community Transport, operating route 455 to Purley. 8494 was acquired by Abellio in September 2011. *Liam Farrer-Beddall*

8114 (KX06LYT) was one of seven Pointer Darts acquired by Abellio in 2011. Three of this batch, 8114 included, were allocated to Hayes for use on the U9 which was taken over from Arriva the Shires. It is on this route that 8114 is seen, having just departed Uxbridge Station. *Liam Farrer-Beddall*

The Covid-19 pandemic of 2020/2021 created the need for extra space to help bus companies adhere to social distancing rules introduced by the Government. 8037 (BU05HFX) was used as a driver rest room at Putney Bridge Station. *Liam Farrer-Beddall*

LONDON SOVEREIGN

On 3 March 2011, the Transdev London operation was divided into two separate operating companies. At this time London United was sold to the RATP Group, with London Sovereign remaining under Transdev ownership, who partnered with Veolia. The new company retained the London Sovereign name and operated from garages in Harrow and Edgware. The new operation saw a number of Plaxton Pointer bodied Dennis Dart SLFs transfer from Transdev. These were DPS1/2, 511-4/6-9, 521-4/6/7/9, 531-4/6, 543/4/6/7/8, 599, 627-30/2-40.

TD2 (LN51KXM) arrived in January 2014 for use as a driver training vehicle. Originating with Metroline as DLD206, TD2 is seen entering Edgware bus station. *Liam Farrer-Beddall*

DP6 (S306MKH) was acquired from London United in June 2011 and was put to use as a driver training vehicle from Edgware. A few months later, in September, DPS599 and DPS627 were also converted to driver training vehicles. The latter vehicle was later renumbered TD3 in March 2014.

The batch of DPS500s did not last long with London Sovereign. The summer of 2011 saw the arrival of forty-three AD Enviro 200s, divided between the two garages. At this time the DPS500s were returned off lease or sold to Ensign. The fleet of DPS600s were retained by London Sovereign, many of which were undergoing a refurbishment.

A second-hand Plaxton Pointer bodied Dart SLF was acquired from Metroline in January 2014. Registered LN51KXM, this 10.1m saloon was added to the driver training fleet and was allocated rolling stock number TD2. It was new to Metroline as DLD206.

The London Sovereign operation was short lived, being acquired by the RATP-DEV Group in March 2014. The Company came under common management with London United, and fleet developments after this date can be found under the London United heading.

TOWER TRANSIT

First London sold its London operations on 22 June 2013, the main business being divided between Metroline and newly formed Tower Transit, owned by Australian based Tower Systems. Tower Transit took over First London's garages at Atlas Road, Lea Interchange and Westbourne Park. The new operator retained the former First London fleet numbers.

It may be recalled from the First London section that First purchased a large volume of Marshall Capital bodied Dennis Dart SLF saloons. After the collapse of Marshall, First purchased a sizable batch of Caetano Nimbus bodied Transbus Darts. Examples of both types were inherited by Tower Transit.

Four Marshall Capital bodied Dart SLFs were taken into stock by Tower Transit. The first two measured 10.2m and were numbered DML41424/5 (LN51DWH and LN51DWJ). The other two were shorter 9.3m DM class saloons. Registered LN51DUA and LN51DUH, they were numbered DM41444 and DM41445 respectively. These were used as driver training vehicles.

A pair of Marshall Capital bodied Dart SLFs were acquired from First London in 2013 for use as driver training vehicles. The second of the pair, DML41425 (LN51DWJ), is seen passing through Archway.

A similar number of Caetano Nimbus bodied Darts were taken into stock. The vehicles concerned were numbered DMC42515 to DMC42518, and carried registration marks LK03NKH/J/L/M.

Eight Plaxton Pointer bodied Dennis Dart SLF saloons were acquired by Tower Transit between 2013 and 2015. The first three arrived in November 2013, acquired to cover an increase in PVR on route 308. These vehicles were registered LG02FFP, FFR and FGO and had previously operated with London United as DPS646/7/65. Tower Transit numbered them DP42600 to DP42602. The next two arrived in May 2014. KP02PUF and KP02PVO were new to Armchair and were allotted rolling stock numbers DP42603/4. January 2015 saw the arrival of the next pair, again originating with Armchair. KP02PWN/O followed on from the 2014 arrivals as DP42605 and DP42606. The final saloon arrived in April 2015 registered KU02YTZ, taking fleet number DP42607. DP42603-7 were used as driver training vehicles. All eight were acquired from Dawson Rentals and were allocated to Lea Interchange.

DP42606 (KP02PWO) represents the small batch of Plaxton Pointer bodied Darts acquired by Tower Transit between 2013 and 2015. It is seen on driver training duties passing Walthamstow Central bus station. *Matthew Wharmby*

SOURCES

The London Bus – Various issues (London Bus Traction Society)

Websites:
London Bus Routes (www.londonbuses.co.uk)
Ian's Bus Stop (www.countrybus.org)